Motivating Reading and Writing
in Diverse Classrooms

NCTE Research Report No. 28

Motivating Reading and Writing in Diverse Classrooms

Social and Physical Contexts in a Literature-Based Program

Lesley Mandel Morrow
Rutgers University

National Council of Teachers of English
1111 W. Kenyon Road, Urbana, IL 61801-1096

Production Editors: Michael Greer, Jamie Hutchinson

Copy Editor: Kurt Kessinger

Interior Book Design: Tom Kovacs for TGK Design

Cover Design: Barbara Yale-Read

NCTE Stock Number: 15624-3050

Library of Congress Cataloging-in-Publication Data

Morrow, Lesley Mandel.
    Motivating reading and writing in diverse classrooms : social and physical contexts in a literature-based program / Lesley Mandel Morrow.
        p. cm.—(NCTE research report, ISSN 0085-3739 ; no. 28)
    Includes bibliographical references and index.
    ISBN 0-8141-1562-4
    1. Language arts (Elementary)—Social aspects—United States. 2. Literature—Study and teaching (Elementary)—Social aspects—United States. 3. Active learning—United States. 4. Multicultural education—United States.   I. Title.   II. Series.
PE1011.N295   no. 28
[LB1576]
428'.007 s—dc20
[372.6]   96-9055
                                                                                   CIP

Contents

Acknowledgments

The investigation reported above was funded by an Elva Knight Research Grant from International Reading Association, a National Council of Teachers of English Research Foundation Award, the Gannett Foundation, and Rutgers University Graduate School of Education's Research Scholar's Grant Program. A special thank you to the National Reading Research Center for their support for the project and continued interest in my work. Material contributions were made by Scholastic Books, *Highlights for Children, Ranger Rick Magazine, Cricket Magazine,* and Harper & Row Junior Books.

I would like to extend gratitude to the superintendent, assistant superintendent, reading specialist, building principals, teachers, parents, and children in the schools where the research was carried out. My appreciation is given to the many Rutgers University students who acted as research assistants during this project. Thanks to the NCTE Publications Board for accepting my work and to Marlo Welshons and Jamie Hutchinson at NCTE for helping with the acceptance and publication process. A special thank you to Evelyn Sharkey and William Firestone for their help with the qualitative portion of the study. In addition, thank you to Jeffrey Smith and William Dolphin for their assistance with the design and analyses of the quantitative data. Thank you to Sandy Chubrick, who formatted the monograph and to Anne Stinson for proofreading.

Portions of this monograph derive from the research report, "The Impact of a Literature-based Program on Literacy Achievement, Use of Literature, and Attitudes of Children from Minority Backgrounds," 1992, *Reading Research Quarterly, 27*(3). The author thanks the *Quarterly* and its publisher, the International Reading Association, for permission to adapt and to reprint portions of that report in this monograph.

1 Introduction

From the instructional perspective of integrating the language arts, children develop literacy through active engagement in authentic experiences with tasks that are meaningful and functional for them. Authentic experiences develop through using children's literature, newspapers, and magazines as the main source and springboard of their literacy activities. Learning takes place within rich literacy environments created specifically to encourage social collaboration during periods devoted to independent reading and writing. Instruction includes strategies planned to integrate literacy learning within different content areas throughout the school day, and it emphasizes learning that is self-regulated through student choice. Teachers and children share responsibility for deciding instructional strategies, activities, and materials (Bergeron, 1990; Goodman, 1989a, 1989b; Morrow, 1992; Teale, 1984).

From the engagement perspective described by Alverman and Guthrie (1993), reading programs should develop engaged readers. Engaged readers are (1) motivated to read voluntarily for pleasure and information; (2) able to use multiple strategies and skills (word analysis and comprehension) to read and understand independently; (3) able to use background information to gain knowledge from new material, then transfer and apply it to new contexts; and (4) able to approach literacy learning socially by soliciting the help of others in order to gain competency. For literacy instruction, the engagement perspective suggests an emphasis on developing a child who not only has strategic skills, but also will be motivated to read for pleasure as well as information. It also means that programs should provide social settings for learning.

The research described in this monograph included the design of a literature-based program that incorporated elements from both an integrated language arts approach and the engagement perspective. The program elements involved (1) the design of literacy centers which created rich literacy environments within classrooms by providing chil-

1

dren with a wide variety of activity choices; (2) pleasurable, teacher-guided literacy strategies that offered models for children to participate independent of the teacher; and (3) reading and writing periods during which children could select participation with others in any of several different literacy activities. These reading and writing periods, referred to as social collaborative reading and writing periods, referred to as Literacy Center Time (LCT), allowed for student choice in activities and time to practice skills learned in a social learning setting. The three elements included the use of children's literature as the main source for learning and, therefore, will be referred to as a literature-based program throughout this monograph.

Purpose of the Study

The purpose of this study was to determine if the literacy achievement, use of literature, and attitudes toward reading of children from diverse backgrounds could be positively affected by a literacy program that emphasized enjoyable experiences with literature. The program was used in partnership with more traditional basal instruction including explicit skill development. This design provided a balanced approach for literacy instruction. The investigation was carried out over an entire school year with children from diverse backgrounds. The study sought to determine what impact, if any, literature-based reading and writing with a social collaborative component would have on (a) children's comprehension as demonstrated by oral and written story retellings and performance on a probed recall test, (b) children's ability to create original oral and written stories with well-formed story structures, (c) children's language complexity and vocabulary development, (d) children's performance on a standardized reading test, (e) attitudes of teachers and children toward using literature in the reading program, and (f) the performance of children involved in a home- and school-based component as compared with the performance of children involved solely in a school-based component.

This quantitative portion of the study sought to determine achievement effects of the literature-based program. However, the program's design raised additional issues for inquiry. The quantitative data gathered in the study did not explore the processes by which the program achieved its effects nor the full range of outcomes. Neither did the

quantitative data address certain questions raised by teachers who are often reluctant to allow such periods because they question the value of social collaborative Literacy Center Time (LCT) during which students self-select materials. There are teachers, for instance, who believe that children do not engage in serious learning without direct instruction. Many teachers are especially concerned that literature-based programs may be inappropriate for children who have difficulty learning, who are considered "at risk," or who have other special needs. Their concerns have been compounded by the suggestion that direct instruction is the most effective strategy for helping such students acquire acceptable skills in reading, writing, and oral language (Delpit, 1988).

To explore these issues, a qualitative analysis from the social collaborative portion of the literary program was conducted simultaneously with the experimental study. The social and learning processes that took place were directly observed and videotaped. Analysis of the data thus gathered revealed a wider range of outcomes than was measured in a quantitative manner, as well as specific similarities and differences among children of different ethnic groups, "ability" levels, and special education classifications. Such qualitative research can both triangulate the results of experimental studies and suggest possible outcomes that might not have been tested in the original experimental design.

Format for the Monograph

Chapter 1 begins with the theoretical background and an extensive literature review concerning issues surrounding the topics at hand. The review includes research on motivation, the effect of physical classroom settings on student behavior, the benefits of using literature in the literacy program, the importance of social, collaborative literacy experiences in motivating reading and writing, and the importance for developing voluntary readers.

Chapter 2 describes the subjects in the study and the methods and procedures used with students in the treatment and control classrooms.

Chapter 3 discusses measures used to collect the quantitative data that dealt with literacy achievement and use of literature. The research design and results of statistical analyses are presented in this chapter as well.

Chapter 4 details the methods and procedures used to collect the qualitative information concerning the attitudes of students and teachers' attitudes toward the literature-based program. The chapter discusses how observational data were gathered regarding social behavior during collaborative literacy periods. Finally, the results of the qualitative analysis are reported.

Chapter 5 reflects upon both the quantitative and qualitative results of the study with implications for classroom practice.

2 A Framework for the Study: Literature Review and Theoretical Framework

The literature-based program designed for this study had the following components: (1) a rich literacy environment, including classroom literacy centers; (2) regular teacher-guided literature activities designed to promote enjoyment and provide a model for children to emulate; (3) self-directed periods for independent reading and writing during which children could collaborate socially; and (4) time for children to perform completed tasks. This framework for literacy instruction was guided by Holdaway's (1979) developmental literacy theory and Cambourne's (1988) theory of learning as it applies to literacy. As such, it provided children with opportunities to (a) observe demonstrations of literacy behavior by adults who read both to them and to themselves; (b) enjoy the support of adults who collaborated or interacted with them socially, who had high expectations for their success, and who offered constructive feedback during their interactions; (c) practice skills in their independent reading and writing that they had been taught earlier; and (d) share literature-based experiences with others through a wide variety of activities such as reading stories they had written and presenting puppet shows based on stories they had read. During social collaborative Literacy Center Times, children participated in reading and writing, took responsibility for their own learning by deciding how to spend each period, and engaged in approximations as they tried new activities, made mistakes, and learned from them.

Teale (1982) views the development of early literacy as the result of children's involvement in reading and writing activities mediated by more literate others. Further, it is the social interaction in these activities that gives them so much significance in the child's development. Not only does interaction teach children the societal functions and conventions of reading and writing, but it also helps them link reading with enjoyment and satisfaction and thus increases their desire to engage in literacy activities. Teale's emphasis on the social aspects of reading development reflects Vygotsky's (1978) more general theory of intellec-

5

tual development—that higher mental functions really are internalized social relationships. It also reflects Piaget's (Piaget & Inhelder, 1969) theory that literacy develops best in an atmosphere that encourages a youngster's social and collaborative interaction with peers through exploration, experimentation, and negotiation.

Motivation Theory

Asked to set priorities for topics of research in the 1990s, a large sample of classroom teachers ranked motivating children to want to read and write high on their list (O'Flahavan, Gambrell, Stahl, & Alverman, 1992). One of the major goals of the study at hand was to motivate children to want to read and write for pleasure and for information. Motivation is indicated by an individual's initiating and sustaining a particular activity, i.e., the tendency to return to and continue working on a task with sustained engagement (Maehr, 1976; Wittrock, 1986). A motivated reader chooses to read on a regular basis and for many different reasons. Researchers have found that experiences which afford students the opportunity for success, challenge, choice, and social collaboration are likely to promote motivation.

To foster success, a learning environment must enable a student to perceive the challenge in the activity at hand as one that he or she can accomplish. When the task has been completed, the student must perceive success (Ford, 1992; McCombs, 1989; Spaulding, 1992; Turner, 1992). Tasks are appropriate only if they are perceived to be challenging, that is, not too hard and not too easy. When children view a task as too easy, they become disinterested; if they view a task as too difficult, they become frustrated. Intrinsic motivation is enhanced when individuals see themselves as competent or successful in challenging situations (Rodin, Rennert, & Solomon, 1980; Spaulding, 1992).

Letting children choose specific literacy activities in which to participate gives them a sense of responsibility and control over a situation. Like challenge and success, self-selection of tasks instills intrinsic motivation (Morrow, 1992; Turner, 1992). Finally, opportunities for social collaboration also nurture motivation. Give children the opportunity to engage in learning through collaboration with a teacher or with peers, and they are more intrinsically motivated and likely to get more done than if they work alone (Brandt, 1990; Oldfather, 1993). Recent investigations by Gambrell, et al. (1993, 1995), also support the findings of the other research reviewed here: that challenge, choice, and collaboration tend to motivate children to read and write.

Rationale for Components of a Literature-Based Program

Creating Literacy Centers in Classrooms

Classroom literacy centers are an important program component in the study reported here, and their design and use follow a well-developed rationale.

We have learned much from observing home environments in which children have learned to read before entering school and without direct instruction. Parents in such homes tend to read to their children, read often themselves, support their children's literacy activities, and routinely maintain and use materials for reading and writing (Durkin, 1974–1975; Taylor, 1983; Teale, 1984). In their theories and philosophies, some of the earliest students of child development emphasized the importance of physical environment in learning and literacy development. Pestalozzi (Rusk & Scotland, 1979) and Froebel (1974) described real-life environments in which learning flourished among young children. Both recognized how the use of appropriate manipulative materials could foster literacy development. Montessori (1965) described a carefully prepared classroom environment intended to promote independent learning and recommended that each material object in that environment be imbued with its specific learning objective. The objectives and materials she recommended were more highly structured than those of either Pestalozzi or Froebel, both of whom allowed more natural settings and situations for learning.

Piaget (Piaget & Inhelder, 1969) found that children acquire knowledge by interacting with the world, through the environment in which they live. Educational interpreters of his theories generally involve children in problem-solving situations which allow them to assimilate new experiences into what they already know. Learning takes place, they maintain, as the child interacts with peers and adults in social settings and conducive environments (Vygotsky, 1978). Ideally, settings are oriented to real-life situations, and materials are chosen that give children the chance to explore and experiment.

Dewey (1916) probably would have supported Piagetian educational settings, although he also stressed interdisciplinary approaches to education through the integration of content-area learning. Maintaining and using materials in subject-area centers within a classroom are a means of encouraging such interest and learning.

Based on these earlier approaches and beliefs, any classroom designed to provide an environment rich in literacy and in opportunities for its development will offer an abundance of materials for reading, writing, and oral language activities. Most of these materials will be housed in a classroom literacy center, and literacy development will be integrated with the content-area teaching reflected in materials available in content-area learning centers. Materials and settings throughout the classroom will be designed to emulate real-life experiences and make literacy especially meaningful to children. They will be based on information the children already possess, and they will be functional, demonstrating to children a need and purpose for literacy activities.

Careful attention to a classroom's physical design contributes to the success of an instructional program. Preparing a classroom's physical environment is often overlooked in planning instruction. Teachers and curriculum developers tend to concentrate on pedagogical and interpersonal factors, but give little consideration to the spatial context in which teaching and learning occur. They direct their energies toward varying teaching strategies while the classroom setting remains relatively unchanged. Unfortunately, when program and environment are not coordinated, "setting deprivation" often results, a situation in which physical environment fails to support the activities and needs of students (Spivak, 1973). The learning environment is often considered mere "background" or "scenery" for teaching and learning.

Fortunately, there is a better way to view both an environment for teaching and learning, and the teacher's role in creating it. It begins with the recognition by teachers that physical setting has an active and pervasive influence on their own activities and attitudes, as well as on those of the children in their classrooms. Those teachers then follow through on that realization with appropriate and purposeful physical arrangement of furniture, careful selection of materials, and increased attention to the aesthetic qualities of their classrooms to provide a setting conducive to teaching and learning (Loughlin & Martin, 1987; Morrow, 1990; Phyfe-Perkins, 1979; Rivlin & Weinstein, 1984). Spatial arrangements alone affect children's classroom behavior. Field (1980) observed that rooms partitioned into smaller spaces facilitated peer and verbal interaction, fantasy, and associative and cooperative play more effectively than did rooms with large open spaces. Moore (1986) found that children in purposefully arranged rooms demonstrated more creative productivity, greater use of language-related activities, more engaged and exploratory behavior, and more social interaction and cooperation than did children in randomly or poorly defined settings. Introducing thematic play materials into the dramatic play area of a laboratory playroom and of a preschool classroom resulted in more elaborate and longer play sequences among children (Dodge & Frost, 1986; Woodward, 1984). Pelligrini (1980) found that incorporating dramatic props into the block center elicited more imaginative language than did playing with blocks alone. Other research has indicated that basing the enrichment and design of dramatic play areas on themes studied in classrooms can increase more general literacy activity and enhance literacy skills (Morrow, 1990; Neuman & Roskos, 1992).

A classroom literacy center is essential in giving children immediate and enjoyable access to literature. Its usefulness and positive influence in the classroom show up most dramatically during periods of independent reading and writing. Well-designed classroom literacy centers have been found to increase significantly the number of children who choose to participate in literary activities during free-choice times (Morrow, 1992; Morrow & Weinstein, 1986). The effort of creating a literacy center with an inviting atmosphere is rewarded by the increased interest of children who participate in the activities offered there (Huck, 1976). The availability and use of the center represent and support the notion that concepts about books and print are acquired when children are exposed to printed materials and given adequate time to explore and experiment with them. Bissett (1969) found that children in classrooms that included their own collections of literature read and looked at books 50 percent more often than did children whose classrooms housed no such collections.

Specific design characteristics of classroom literacy centers in nursery schools and kindergartens have been shown to correlate positively with the number of children who use those areas during free-choice periods. Conversely, it has been found that children given free-choice opportunities to do so tend not to use poorly designed literacy centers.

Clearly, the physical features of a classroom literacy center are important if children are to be induced to use them voluntarily (Rosenthal,
1973; Morrow, 1992).

Teacher-Modeled Literature Activities

A second component of the program at the center of this study is the
teacher's role as model for the children in the use and enjoyment of literature and of activities based on that literature. Teachers model skill
activities and the use of materials in traditional whole-group settings so
that students will be able to reinforce and practice skills during periods
of collaborative reading and writing.

Children's literature is an important source for literacy instruction in
early childhood classrooms (Cullinan, 1987). Research has shown that
introducing and using literature with young children correlates positively with development of sophisticated language structures, including
vocabulary and syntax (Chomsky, 1972). Cullinan (1987) suggested
that language development correlates with reading success, and that
both can be improved by regular use of children's literature. Children
exposed to literature accumulate background knowledge not only about
the content at hand but also about how language works and how written
language differs from spoken. These children often show an early interest in reading; they tend to learn to read early and to enjoy reading
(Durkin, 1974–75). More recent research has confirmed the importance
of providing children with daily opportunities to experience literature
in active and pleasurable ways—by reading and telling stories to children, for instance; dealing with stories through literal, interpretive, and
critical discussions; integrating literature into themes being studied
throughout the curriculum; and encouraging children to share books
they have read, to respond to literature through written and oral language, and to participate regularly in social periods set aside for reading and writing (Hoffman, Roser, & Farest, 1988; Morrow, O'Connor,
& Smith, 1990).

Reading aloud to children has become an important practice with
beneficial outcomes. It is apparently not the read-aloud event alone that
yields positive results so much as it is the verbal interaction between
adult and child during the experience (Morrow, O'Connor, & Smith,
1990). A read-aloud event involves social relationships among people:
teachers and students, parents and children, authors and readers. Be-

cause reading stories to children is a social activity, children almost never encounter simply an oral rendering of text. Rather, the author's words are augmented and shaped by the interpretation and interaction of the adult reader and child as they cooperatively negotiate and reconstruct meaning from text (Teale & Sulzby, 1986). Researchers agree that what the adult and child talk about in the interaction holds the key to the effect of storybook reading. Vygotsky (1978) describes cognitive development as growing out of social interactions. From that perspective, the importance of read-aloud events is their social interactiveness, with the adult serving initially as mediator between text and child and providing the opportunity for both adult and child to make or take meaning from the text.

Felesenthal's (1989) findings indicate that using children's literature offers an ideal opportunity to develop critical reading. Research indicates that reading is a constructive process. Readers come to texts with backgrounds of knowledge that help them construct meaning from the print before them. Further, readers construct meaning as they interact with peers and adults when discussing stories (Jett-Simpson, 1989). The content of children's literature lends itself particularly well to drawing on background knowledge and to interaction with peers and adults to help construct meaning from text, as in story discussions, role playing, and retelling. Skillful use of a Directed Reading/Listening/ Thinking Activity (DLTA or DRTA) is another way to provide challenge, choice, success, and collaboration in experiencing literature. Its format consists of prereading questions, discussion, prediction, reading (either to or by the children), and post-reading discussion, all focusing generally on a specific objective or purpose for listening or reading. The procedure has been found to improve children's story comprehension (Morrow, 1984).

Using such props as feltboards, puppets, and roll movies to retell a story, with or without a copy of the story in hand, not only actively involves the child in story reconstruction, but also helps develop comprehension, sense of story structure, and oral language ability (Gambrell, Kapinus, & Koskinen, 1991; Morrow, 1985; Spiegel & Whaley, 1980). Other researchers have found that dramatic play with story props can improve story production and comprehension, including recall of details and ability to sequence and interpret (Mandler & Johnson, 1977; Saltz & Johnson, 1974).

Questions have been raised concerning the efficacy of literature-based process instruction with children of diverse backgrounds. It has been suggested that process approaches are inappropriate for some minority children because those processes tend to skirt direct instruction of the information and skills needed to acquire what is considered acceptable forms of reading, writing, and oral language. Minority children, it is said, need to acquire those mainstream forms if they are to compete and succeed in the larger culture in which they live, that is the culture outside their homes and neighborhoods. It has also been suggested that classrooms using exclusively process-oriented strategies, such as learning in small groups through self-directed peer tutoring and collaboration, may be inappropriate for some of these students. Because they are typically more accustomed to explicit instructions than to open-ended situations, the suggestion continues, children from minority backgrounds may behave inappropriately because they are unsure about what is expected of them (Delpit, 1986, 1988).

Concerns have also been voiced that literature-based instruction may not benefit children from diverse cultural backgrounds. Many such youngsters have not been exposed to the literature traditionally taught in American classrooms. Others may be acquainted only with the literatures of their own cultural heritage, and thus find "traditional" American stories and responses to literature difficult to understand (Michaels, 1984; Scallon & Scallon, 1984).

Other researchers who have studied these problems generally agree that it is necessary to (a) value and rejoice in the home cultures of children from diverse backgrounds, (b) be sensitive to the sense of identity and self-esteem inherent in cultural values, (c) plan instructional strategies that promote the understanding of diverse cultures so that all youngsters can benefit from school, and (d) recognize how important it is for all children to learn to deal with literature and literacy skills used in the larger culture in which they live. This will empower them to succeed in that larger culture while continuing to recognize and treasure the special values in their own native cultures (Delpit, 1991).

Social Contexts for Motivating Reading and Writing

A third major component of the program under study is the engagement of children in socially interactive settings in order to motivate their desire to read and write both for pleasure and for information. The language arts perspective, the engagement perspective, and research on motivation theory all point to the importance of collaboration and inter- action with adults and peers as an important factor in literacy learning. To promote literacy development in the classroom, this theoretical con- struct must be translated and incorporated into practice. Children in the program under study, therefore, had multiple and frequent opportuni- ties to interact socially during collaborative periods for reading and writing.

Cooperative and collaborative work which includes social interac- tion in small groups has been shown to increase both achievement and productivity in children (Johnson & Johnson, 1987; Slavin, 1983). Yager, Johnson, & Johnson (1985) posit two important elements in the dynamics of cooperative learning: oral interaction among students and heterogeneity among group members. Their findings indicate that co- operative learning succeeds because it allows children to explain mate- rial to each other, to listen to each other's explanations, and to arrive at joint understandings of what they have shared. Cooperative learning also enables "more capable peers" to offer support to others. Cazden (1986) notes that peer interaction allows students to attempt a range of roles usually denied to them by traditional student-teacher structures. Citing Vygotsky's theory (1978), Forman and Cazden (1985) also con- clude that interactional transformation can occur among peers when one student observes, guides, and corrects as another performs a task. The students accomplish more together than either could accomplish alone; working in peer dyads allows for learning opportunities similar to tutoring. Forman and Cazden's discussion reflects both Dewey's (1916) argument that children engaged in task-oriented dialogue with peers can reach higher levels of understanding than when teachers present information didactically, and Piaget's (Piaget & Inhelder, 1969) suggestion that childhood peers serve as resources for one another in cognitive development.

Less dependence on the teacher seems to motivate intrinsic learning (Wood, 1990). Children who ordinarily work alone choose to collabo- rate in cooperative settings, some even forming friendships. Working in cooperative groups apparently fosters greater acceptance of differences among students (Slavin, 1990). Cooperative learning can succeed even when high and low achievers work together; furthermore it encourages positive relations among children from different racial and ethnic backgrounds (Augustine, Gruber, & Hanson, 1989; Kagan, et al., 1985; Morrow, 1992). Finally, children with such special needs as physical disabilities, emotional handicaps, and learning difficulties are more likely to be accepted by other children in cooperative learning settings than in traditional classrooms (Johnson & Johnson, 1981; Lew, Mesch, Johnson, & Johnson, 1986; Morrow, 1992).

The suggestion has been forwarded, however, that because of cultural and linguistic differences, some youngsters may not be able to function effectively when they participate in small-group activities (Delpit, 1991). In response to that concern, it has been positively demonstrated that social context as an environmental factor can positively affect the literacy learning of children from diverse backgrounds and ability, including those identified as at-risk and average achievers as well as the gifted and those children who represent diverse races and cultures. Studies with at-risk kindergartners and children from diverse backgrounds in first, second, and third grades found that such socially interactive strategies as daily storybook reading, story retelling, use of literature manipulatives, and periods of independent reading and writing helped experimental groups score better than control groups on comprehension, retelling, and extent of voluntary participation in literacy activities (Morrow, 1992; Morrow, O'Connor, & Smith, 1990). Social interaction between adult and child and among children themselves seemed to be a major factor in the positive outcomes.

A Rationale for Creating Voluntary Readers and Writers

Besides concern for literacy achievement this study was attempting to develop engaged readers and writers who read and write voluntarily for pleasure and for information. What justifies acute pedagogical attention to the value, characteristics, and extent of voluntary reading and writing, especially in a child's earlier years? Steven Spielberg (1987) said that in such reading "We reignite our romance with the written word." That statement captures the major thrust of the investigation at hand. Few Americans doubt that voluntary reading and writing are at once practical, beneficial, and cherished as joyous privileges in life. Yet, little or no formal attention is given to their promotion and development. Indeed, some critics observe that undue emphasis on skills in early instruction can even discourage the acts of reading and writing by personal choice. Because a thoroughly democratic society depends on the cultivation and practice of literacy, children's voluntary pursuit of literacy should rank high as a goal among both parents and teachers—at home and in school. Developing as voluntary readers and writers, children learn to associate these activities with pleasure. They enjoy looking at books and eventually reading them. They tend to read and write more, which in turn leads to improved literacy ability. Voluntary, recreational reading and writing must be incorporated as an integral part of the total developmental literacy program so that children will decide on their own to spend portions of their time reading and writing or participating in other literacy-related activities.

In a 1984 report to Congress entitled *Books in our Future,* Daniel Boorstin, at the time Librarian of Congress, warned that alliterates—individuals who can read but choose not to do so—constitute a threat at least equal to that of illiterates in a democratic tradition built on books and reading. The practice or absence of voluntary reading, he wrote, "will determine the extent of self-improvement and enlightenment, the ability to share wisdom and the delights of our civilization, and our capacity for intelligent self-government" (p. iv).

Teaching people to read and write is certainly the most pervasive goal of American schooling. It is all but impossible to identify a goal more basic or traditional. It is remarkable, therefore, that so little instructional attention is paid to developing voluntary readers and writers—especially in the early years of schooling—that is, youngsters who will choose to read and write widely and often on their own.

Among other things, *Becoming a Nation of Readers* (1985) notes that learning to read requires motivation or desire to read, requires practice in order to develop proficiency, and must be a lifelong pursuit in order to maintain fluency. The components of a voluntary reading and writing program such as that outlined in the study at hand seek to motivate an interest in and desire to read and write; encourage free reading and writing, which provides practice for proficiency; and encourage continued literacy development throughout the grades, both in school and at home.

The Extent of Voluntary Reading

Unfortunately, it is clear that substantial numbers of children and adults read neither for pleasure nor for information. Studies by Morrow and Weinstein (1986) found that few primary grade children chose to look at books during free-choice time in school, while Greaney (1980) found that fifth grade students spent only 5.4 percent of their leisure time engaged in reading, and that 22 percent of them did not read at all. In similar studies, Walberg and Tsai (1984), Greaney & Hegarty (1987), and Anderson, Wilson, and Fielding (1988), all found that many children choose not to read very much in their spare time.

It has been hypothesized that forms of electronic equipment which have been introduced over the years may be diverting youths' attention away from books. However, comparative studies between television viewing and leisure reading have not substantiated the general hypothesis that electronic entertainment brings a decline in voluntary reading. Research data overall are simply inconclusive. Both heavy and light readers are among viewers who watch a substantial amount of television, and there are both heavy and light readers who report watching little television. Studies tend to confirm the belief that viewing television does not itself detract from reading books (Childers & Ross, 1973; Neuman, 1980).

A second factor sometimes suggested for the low prevalence of voluntary reading is the fact that many instructional programs still do not provide ample opportunity for students to read for enjoyment in school (Lamme, 1976; Spiegel, 1981). This possibility has been bolstered somewhat by reports from schools in which recreational reading, or reading for enjoyment, has been incorporated as a regular element into instructional programs. The systematic promotion of pleasurable literary activities in such programs does indeed seem to have enhanced enthusiasm and fostered positive student attitudes toward reading (Irving, 1980; Manley & Simon, 1980; Morrow, 1992).

In spite of that fact, most schools still generally gauge the success of their reading programs not by the personal reading habits of their students, but by "successful" scores on standardized reading tests (Irving, 1980; Spiegel, 1981). General comprehension skills, rather than application of such skills to personal use and benefit, are commonly considered the ultimate goal of a reading program. Children are taught to read but not to develop the habit of reading. Ironically, as Holdaway (1979) points out, schools spend a great deal of time teaching literacy skills, then leave little room for children to practice those skills. Thus, it is not surprising that substantial numbers of children choose not to read and write. Children's reading habits develop early in life, no later than sixth grade. If schools do not deliberately and thoughtfully attract children to reading during earlier years, voluntary reading may never become a life-long habit.

Benefits Associated with Voluntary Reading

Studies which have documented the fact that many children spend little time in voluntary reading have also revealed converse evidence of strong relationships between leisure reading and reading achievement (Greaney, 1980). A study by Anderson, Wilson, and Fielding (1988) asked children to record the number of minutes they spent reading outside school. Their time spent reading correlated positively with their reading achievement. The study revealed that children who scored at the 90th percentile on a reading test spent an average of five times as many minutes per day reading books as do children at the 50th percentile, and more than 200 times as many minutes per day reading books as children at the 10th percentile. Children whose voluntary reading is substantial also demonstrate positive attitudes towards reading (Greaney, 1980; Morrow, 1992). It seems apparent that an element of personal motivation in voluntary reading contributes to greater interest and skill development (Irving, 1980). But, a study of kindergarten children found that those youngsters strongly interested in books were also rated by their teachers as displaying high performance in fine motor control, social and emotional maturity, good work habits, and general excellence in school achievement. They also performed well on a standardized reading readiness test (Morrow, O'Connor, & Smith, 1990).

An obvious conclusion follows from the cultural, political, moral, and educational factors involved in reading frequently and widely on one's own: the well-educated person chooses to read because it is socially, individually, and educationally beneficial to do so. We teach youngsters to read so they can participate fully in a civilized society. For such participation, they must become readers by choice, not by coercion. How else will they or our society realize all the benefits that ability to read brings with it?

The promotion of voluntary reading and writing, then, is appropriate among children from their very earliest years. As educators, we need to study and promote the techniques of developing voluntary readers and writers at least to the same extent as we explore the process of training children to decipher the printed page (Morrow, 1986).

Characteristics of Voluntary Readers

Many studies have found that a rich literacy environment at home contributes most significantly to children's voluntary reading and interest in literature. Parents with children who are early voluntary readers have themselves served as reading models for their children by reading often in their leisure time, whether they read novels, magazines, newspapers, or work-related materials. Other characteristics of homes in which children were voluntary readers became evident. They tended to house greater numbers of books, and the books could be found in many different rooms, including playrooms, kitchens, and children's bedrooms. Parents of voluntary readers often took their children to libraries. They read to their children daily. They enforced television rules, including selective viewing and limitations on the amount of viewing allowed (Clark, 1976; Clay, 1976; Durkin, 1974–75; Morrow, 1997; Taylor, 1983; Teale, 1984).

Children who are voluntary readers demonstrate distinct characteristics themselves. Greaney (1980), Long & Henderson (1973), and Whitehead, Capey, & Maddren (1975) all report that such readers tend to be girls who are high achievers in school and particularly successful in reading performance. The younger ones among them tend to spend playtime at home writing and drawing as well as looking at books, whereas children who show a low interest prefer playing outdoors with toys. Children who demonstrate an early interest in books watch less television daily than those who do not. Most of the research reviewed also indicates that voluntary readers and children with strong interest in books score well on reading tests at school.

One study, however (Morrow, 1983), identified a number of children whose interest in books was low, but whose mean percentile scores on a reading readiness test were higher than the average scores of the entire high-interest group. Conversely, some of the children in the high-interest group achieved mean percentile scores on the test similar only to the average for the total low-interest group. The findings of that particular study present an interesting consideration. While it has been generally accepted that school achievement and recreational reading are related, the results of this study indicate that skilled readers are not necessarily voluntary readers. Even though a child demonstrates academic ability when tested, if neither the school nor the home offers a supportive literary environment, the child might not develop voluntary reading habits. On the other hand, a child exposed to literature at home and in school may develop a strong interest in books in spite of lower academic ability as indicated on standardized test scores. Anderson, Wilson, & Fielding (1988) found that children who were in classrooms that promoted voluntary reading read more at home than did children in classrooms which offered little emphasis in that direction. Taylor, Frye, & Maruyama (1990) found that the amount of time spent reading in school contributed significantly to gains in students' reading achievement.

Promoting Voluntary Reading in School

Educators widely agree that encouraging students to develop lifelong, voluntary reading habits is important. Niles wrote in the foreword to *Reading for Pleasure: Guidelines* (Spiegel, 1981): "If we teach children to read, but do not instill the desire to read, what will we have accomplished?" (p. v). If, on the other hand, children learn in an environment that associates reading with pleasure and enjoyment as well as with skill development, they are likely to become voluntary readers. How children live and learn in the classroom ultimately determines whether they will live their lives as literate or alliterate individuals. Irving (1980) contends that "One of the clear points to emerge from research into reading failure is that there was no association between reading and pleasure. The role of teachers in stimulating voluntary reading among children and young people is . . . potentially the most powerful of all adult influences upon the young" (p. 7).

The literature program at the heart of the present study was carried out in partnership with traditional explicit basal reading instruction, allowing children to experience literature pleasurably, positively, and supportively. The program design shaped by the several theories described earlier, derived from the author's earlier research into strategies that tend to motivate children's voluntary reading. The model for literacy instruction being utilized in this study could be referred to as a balanced approach. It encompasses reading and language arts processes by acknowledging (1) the importance of both form (mechanics, word analysis, etc.) and function (comprehension, purpose, meaning) of the literacy processes and (2) that learning occurs most effectively in a whole-part-whole context. This type of instruction is characterized by meaningful literacy activities that utilize both literature-based and more explicit instructional materials and strategies. This approach should provide children with both the skill and desire to become proficient and lifelong voluntary readers and writers.

The research reported here expanded on past work by carrying a program over an entire school year with children from diverse backgrounds. It also focused on achievement gains, increased use of literature, and improved attitudes towards the program. The nature of social interaction that took place during periods of independent reading and writing are an important component of the observational, qualitative portion of this investigation. One of the major goals of the study was to determine if the treatment creates motivated readers and writers, students who voluntarily choose to read and write.

3 Methods and Procedures Used to Carry Out the Study

Subjects

The subjects were enrolled in nine second grade classrooms in two schools within one school district. They included 72 African American, 62 white, 23 Asian, and 9 Latino children. Two-thirds of the subjects represented minority backgrounds. The black population was made up of African American children, the Hispanic children were from Cuba and Puerto Rico, and the Asians were from Korea, India, and Japan. The distribution of children was similar in each classroom with approximately 10 African American, 8 white, 4 Asian, and 2 Latino in a class of 24. The distribution was so similar because children were bused throughout the district to achieve racial balance in each school. Because the district had been busing for many years, diversity was the norm; children from diverse backgrounds were commonly accepted within the schools.

Complete data were collected for 166 children: 84 boys and 82 girls. Classes were heterogeneously grouped and similar in terms of educational programs. Twenty-two percent of the students in the study had been classified "at risk" as determined by a state regulation that any student who received a Normal Curve Equivalency (NCE) of 34 or less in reading and of 36 or less in language on the California Test of Basic Skills was to be categorized "at risk" and eligible for enrollment in basic-skills classes. Twenty-four percent of the children in the study were eligible for a free-lunch program and considered "disadvantaged." Eligibility for the free-lunch program had also been determined by the state according to formula calculations that included income and number of children per family. The socioeconomic status (SES) of the subjects in the study ranged from middle class to disadvantaged. According to local school officials, children from the various backgrounds were present in each of the SES groups and no background was predominant in any category.

All teachers taking part in the study were female. They averaged 14 years of teaching experience in a range from 6 to 25 years. All classrooms met the following pre-study criteria:

1. Traditional basal readers were the main source of reading instruction, and literature was not an integral part of the regular reading program. Teachers had minimum experience with literature-based strategies.

2. The classrooms did not have well-designed literacy centers.

3. Social collaborative settings for reading and writing were not an integral part of literacy instruction.

The nine classrooms were randomly selected from the two buildings, and students in those classrooms were then randomly assigned to one of three groups, making three classrooms per group: a control group (35 boys and 29 girls) and two experimental groups (E1 and E2). Subjects in the three E1 classrooms (26 boys and 30 girls) received school-based intervention as well as participation in a reading-at-home program; subjects in the three E2 classrooms (23 boys and 23 girls) received school-based intervention only. Subjects in the three control classrooms were instructed in reading as it had been carried out before the study began.

Procedures

The pre-intervention phase of the study began the third week of school, during which comprehension and writing tests, plus use-of-literature and attitude inventories, were administered to all experimental and control children.

Intervention was implemented in the two experimental groups during the first week of October and continued through the following May. Observations were conducted in the experimental rooms once a week during the intervention period. Classes were observed during both basal reading instruction and literature-based activities to ensure that all components of the program under study were being carried out as intended. During the intervention children in the experimental rooms kept records of the books they read in the classroom and those they checked out to read at home. At the beginning of May, the measures given prior to intervention were again administered to all children, this time as post-tests.

Nature of the Reading Program Prior to the Treatment

Before the study program described here, the major source for reading instruction in the district had been a basal reader program with accompanying workbook materials. Within that instructional pattern, children were divided into four reading groups per classroom, with assignment to each reading group based on ability. Reading instruction took place five days a week for approximately 1 hour and 30 minutes each day, approximately 7 hours a week. During instructional periods, the teacher met with each of the groups in her classroom, and children read stories from the basal readers. When not being so instructed by their teacher, children carried out seatwork activities consisting mostly of using worksheets from workbooks. When they finished working with basal reading materials during a reading period, children were allowed to read books they had checked out individually from the school library or had selected from a small collection of trade books on a shelf in the classroom itself. Teachers did occasionally read stories to children from sources other than the basal readers, but usually only when there was time left over from basal reading and other activities, not on a regular basis.

The Treatment

The intervention program was intended to complement and extend basal reading instruction using the literature-based program. All experimental classrooms used the basal reading series adopted by the district plus the literature program. To incorporate the added use of literature, however, less time was allotted to basal instruction in the experimental classrooms. The control and experimental groups all spent the same amount of time on reading instruction from October through May, the duration of the research study.

Before carrying out treatment, teachers in the experimental classrooms participated in three half-days of inservice training to become familiar with the program they would be implementing. Each was given a curriculum handbook I had written especially for the instructional program to be studied. It provided a rationale and background for the program, materials needed, and lesson plans for various activities. It also included a section on classroom management, since some of the activities required organizational strategies that teachers might not have used before. Training sessions also included demonstrations, simulations, and time for questions and answers.

The teachers and I also met during the entire intervention period itself: once a week for the first month, twice a week for the second two months, and once a month for the rest of the school year. At these meetings, we discussed problems and concerns ranging from classroom management to skill development. We also shared activities that the teachers had carried out, shared materials that children had created, and suggested to each other how the program might be improved. The school principals and the district reading coordinator also attended our meetings from time to time, demonstrating their support and encouraging the program. Finally, during the entire intervention period research assistants made weekly visits to experimental and control teachers to answer questions, listen to concerns, and provide additional materials if needed.

(It bears repeating here that the balanced approach to literacy instruction used in this study embraces both the form and function of literacy processes and acknowledges the effectiveness of whole-part-whole contexts for learning. In this balanced approach, meaningful literacy activities are being utilized with both literature-based and more explicit instructional materials and strategies, providing children with both the skill and desire to become proficient and lifelong voluntary readers and writers.)

The literature-based portions of reading instruction in the experimental groups included the design of literacy centers in the treatment classrooms, teacher-modeled literature activities, and social collaborative literacy periods for reading and writing for both E1 and E2 groups. The E1 groups also had a parent involvement, home/school connection component. Descriptions of the basic characteristics of each follow:

Classroom Literacy Centers. Literacy centers were created in each of the experimental rooms. Each center was designed for easy accessibility, located in a quiet portion of the room, and defined physically to ensure an atmosphere of privacy. Centers contained regular bookshelves as well as open-faced shelves for displaying featured books with covers showing. Included in each center were five to eight books per child representing three to four grade levels and various genres of children's literature: biographies, picture story books, novels, poetry, newspapers, magazines, and informational books with expository text.

Books representing the children's different cultural backgrounds were also included to demonstrate interest in and respect for diverse heritages, to help inform children about different cultures and cultural values, and to help them identify a sense of their own worth. Because the professional literature on children's preferences in reading is so inconclusive, the centers were stocked with a wide range of genres in the hope of providing at least something for everyone.

Books were rotated on and off the shelves regularly, and each center featured a system for checking out books for home use. Pillows, rugs, stuffed animals, and rocking chairs added comfort to the centers. Literature manipulatives such as feltboards and story-character cutouts, taped stories and headsets, puppets for use in storytelling, and materials for chalk talks and roll movies were readily available. Each center was equipped with an "Author's Spot" supplied with various types of writing paper, booklets, and writing utensils with which children could write stories and make books. Children in the experimental groups also received subscriptions to the magazine *Highlights for Children,* which was sent to their homes once a month for the duration of the study.

Overall, each literacy center demonstrated the importance of literacy by giving it a special, integral place in the classroom. In addition to its accessibility, it also introduced children to literature through several modalities for engaging in active, social, literacy activities.

Teacher-Modeled Literature-Based Activities. Each teacher was given a handbook describing literature-based activities appropriate to the experimental program. Teachers in E1 and E2 classrooms were asked to carry out three literature-based activities each week and to read to children daily, regardless of any other activities they might decide to use. Activities suggested for their use included engaging children in retelling and rewriting stories; in creating original oral and written stories; in storytelling through such techniques as roll movies, felt stories, and chalk talks; in sharing with other children the books they had read; in checking books out; and in having children keep track on index cards of books they had read.

In leading or encouraging activities that involved stories per se, teachers were also urged to emphasize story elements such as plot structure and the distinctive styles of various authors and illustrators. They were asked to include literal, interpretive, and critical issues in literature-based discussions. Activities should include explanations of and discussions about different genres of children's literature, including literature connected to content area subjects such as social studies and science, plus, when appropriate, attention to word recognition and comprehension development. Activities should call attention to the cultural diversity represented by materials in the classroom literacy center. Above all, the activities in their classrooms should emphasize the joy of literature.

Teachers were also asked to include writing as an integral part of the program, especially as it would draw from and add to the literature base underlying all program activities. In great measure, teacher-guided, literature-based activities would provide children with models for emulation in their own self-selected activities.

In the following example from the implemented program, a teacher guides a literature-based activity.

> Mrs. Meechem read the story *A Letter to Amy* (Keats, 1968), and followed it by leading a discussion of the book's illustrations. Jason said while he thought the illustrations looked like real people, he also wondered if the pictures were paintings and not photographs. Mrs. Meechem then pointed out that Ezra Jack Keats illustrates stories with collages, using bits of newspaper, wallpaper, lace, and other materials woven into his paintings. She then read *Green Eggs and Ham* (Seuss, 1960) and drew attention to Dr. Seuss's illustrations. Patrick noted that the cartoon characters Dr. Seuss drew for his books don't look real at all, and sometimes indeed look very silly. Following the two readings, Mrs. Meechem displayed other books by Keats and Dr. Seuss. The children compared illustrations and could easily determine which books were created by which illustrator. Mrs. Meechem set as the theme for the SCL period the study of the styles of authors and illustrators. In doing so, she suggested that children select an author and illustrator as a guide for writing their own story, and use the author and illustrator's style of writing and illustrating as a guide for their own work.

The teacher plays an important role in motivating interest in literature and other materials in the literacy center. She models use of the materials, engages the children in stimulating discussions concerning books read, and by doing so shows how enjoyable these activities can be, as the following example illustrates.

> Mrs. Payton demonstrated how to use a feltboard and cutout characters while reading a story. She asked Roseangela to place

the appropriate figures on the board as she read the book *Are You My Mother?* (Eastman, 1960). To include all the children in the experience, she asked them to make appropriate sounds for animals in the story as Roseangela placed the animal cutouts on the feltboard. At the end of the presentation, the children applauded. Mrs. Payton then suggested that they themselves could follow the same procedure with *Are You My Mother?* and other stories. They could even make their own character cutouts for other stories.

Literacy Center Time (LCT). From three to five times a week, children were given opportunities to choose from a variety of literature-based activities in which to participate. They could read a book, read to a friend, listen to a taped story, tell a story with the feltboard, ask someone to read to them, check out books to take home, write a story, or other appropriate activities. These LCTs gave students unusual latitude, but choices were available only within a framework of rules. For instance, children could choose to work alone or with others, but they were expected to stay with only one or two activities during each thirty-minute independent period. The use of manipulatives had to be accompanied by or related to specific books. Each LCT was intended to emphasize a concept that had already been featured by the teacher, such as story resolution. On-task behavior was a goal for LCT activities. For the purposes of this investigation, "on task" meant that children were to be engaged in an activity that involved reading, writing, or oral language. They could be reading a book, writing a story, performing a puppet show, planning the role-playing of a story, binding a book for a story they had written, or other activity, but they had to be "on task" in their literature-based activity.

During each LCT, the teacher worked as a facilitator, at various times helping children begin their individual or group activities, modeling behaviors as needed, reading books of their own choice with or to children, and sharing manipulatives. Children were expected to record tasks they had accomplished and to share their records of accomplishments with the rest of the class. Following is an illustration of how teachers used their time during a typical LCT.

Mrs. Pelovitz first sat with Patrick, Lewis, James, Tiffany, and Shawna to look at the roll movie they had just created for the story *Mr. Rabbit and the Lovely Present* (1962), written by Charlotte Zolotow and illustrated by Maurice Sendak. She congratulated the group for a job well done, then became the audience when the students insisted on performing a roll movie for her.

At the end of their presentation, she commented that the pictures were "very vivid." James said he didn't know what *vivid* meant, so Mrs. Pelovitz defined the word for him. Before leaving the group, she said, "If Maurice Sendak, the illustrator of this story, were to walk in the door of our room right now, he would think that he had drawn the pictures for the movie."

In the initial stages of social collaborative reading and writing periods teachers established rules because the structure of the LCT was different from any classroom activity in which the children had previously participated. About a month passed before students were able to select activities independently, decide whether to work alone or together, work productively in groups, and stay on task. Montessori's (1965) theory was followed to manage LCT for simultaneous productivity and enjoyment. The theory underlies the following rules which were put to general use during each LCT:

Rules to Follow During Social Cooperative Literacy Center Time

1. Decide who you will work with.

2. Choose a reading or writing activity.

3. Do only one or two activities in a given period.

4. Use materials in or outside of the literacy center.

5. All activities must include reading, writing, or both.

6. Handle materials carefully.

7. Speak in soft voices.

8. Put materials back in their place before taking more.

9. Try new activities you haven't done before.

10. Work with people you haven't worked with before.

11. Stay with a group to complete tasks.

12. Record completed tasks in your log.

13. Be ready to share completed tasks with the class.

In addition to general guidelines, rules for cooperative behavior also governed LCTs:

Helping You to Work in Groups

When Working in Groups ...

> Select a leader to help the group get started.
>
> Give everyone a job.
>
> Share materials.
>
> Take turns talking.
>
> Listen to your friends when they talk.
>
> Respect what others have to say.
>
> Stay with your group.

Helpful Things to Say to Group Members:

> Can I help you?
>
> I like your work.
>
> You did a good job.

Check How Well You Cooperated and Check Your Work.

> Did you say helpful things?
>
> Did you help each other?
>
> Did you share materials?
>
> Did you take turns?
>
> Did you all have jobs?
>
> How well did your jobs get done?
>
> What can we do better next time?

When initiating LCT teachers assigned children to groups, decided which activities they would participate in, and selected leaders to organize each activity. After a few weeks teachers let children sign up for activities and groups before the period began. After participating in assigned groups with assigned tasks, children could make these decisions themselves; they were allowed to choose people with whom to work, pick leaders, and select tasks. To help children select activities, a list of things to do during LCT was posted.

Things to Do During Literacy Center Time

1. Read a book, a magazine, or a newspaper.

2. Read to a friend.

3. Listen to someone read to you.

4. Listen to a taped story while following the words in the book.

5. Use the feltboard with story book and felt characters.

6. Use the roll movie with its story book.

7. Write a story.

8. Draw a picture about a story you read.

9. Make a story you wrote into a book.

10. Make a felt story for a book you read or story you wrote.

11. Write a puppet show and perform it.

12. Make a taped story for a book you read or story you wrote.

13. Check out books to take home and read.

14. Use Activity Cards to select things to do.

(Activity Cards list steps for carrying out activities and thus help children organize their work.)

The role of the teacher during LCT was to model behavior and act as a facilitator as children engage in a variety of literacy activities that were both social and collaborative in nature, such as writing their own stories, or preparing felt characters or roll movies for presenting them. Children could demonstrate comprehension by retelling stories on tape or with puppets, or through dramatic presentations.

Reading at Home. Three of the experimental classes (the E1 group) accompanied the school-based program component with a home-based one. Participating parents attended three training sessions on literature-based activities they could enjoy and share at least twice a week with their youngsters, such as reading to their children, going to the library, sharing books, making books, and providing space for books at home. Parents kept records of the activities they carried out. Of the 56 children in the reading-at-home group, only 38 parents attended training sessions, and most of those parents attended only one of the three sessions. Ten parents attended all three.

Managing the Treatment

The teacher-guided, literature-based activities and LCTs could be woven into the school day in many different ways. A teacher could first lead an activity, then follow it up with an LCT, or the two activities could be carried out at separate times of the day. The teacher could also choose to incorporate literature-based components into her basal reading program. Some teachers scheduled basal reading instruction on two days a week and literature-based components on the other three, then alternated the following week with basal instruction on three days and literature-based on the other two. Other teachers wove the two programs together or scheduled literature-based activities throughout the school day. Whichever approach individual teachers chose, the program was implemented gradually, with some teachers incorporating all elements sooner than others. By the second month, however, all teachers were carrying out all components of the experimental program and seemed comfortable doing so. One factor that allowed implementing the program rather quickly was the fact that literature-based activities were only one piece of their total reading instruction. Teachers needed only to learn the new procedures and allocate time for them, and they continued the rest of their literacy instruction as usual.

Monitoring the Program

Teachers did carry out the program as designed, a fact documented by research assistants who observed classrooms weekly and who took field notes at all visits. Those teachers who were most enthusiastic about the program spent a bit more time on literature-based activities than did other participants. But, overall, our observations, discussions with teachers, and review of their individual logs led us to conclude that all participating classes carried out the minimum number of required activities. That is, all teachers read to children daily, carried out at least three other literature-based activities a week, and provided LCTs three times a week. Differences among the participating teachers in the number of activities and amount of time devoted to the program were minimal because of time constraints in the overall school curriculum.

Control Rooms

Reading instruction in the control group continued as it had in the past, with the basal reader as the main source of instruction. The basal reader program used in the district dated from 1988. The two second-grade books included about twenty-eight selections, eight of which were original pieces of children's literature. As described earlier, most teachers in those classrooms divided students into four reading groups selected on the basis of ability. Children read selections from basal readers and completed worksheets from workbooks. If they completed their basal reading activities before the end of the time allotted to reading instruction, they were allowed to read trade books.

There was some overlap between the kinds of discussion surrounding literature selections in the experimental groups and those suggested by the basals in their section on comprehension. Both the literature-based and the basal programs emphasized literal, interpretive, and critical comprehension skills as well as structural elements of stories.

The literature-based program required the allocation of additional time for reading instruction for the experimental classes. To ensure that this fact did not confound treatment effects, schedules were adjusted between experimental and control classes, equalizing total time devoted to reading instruction. Thus, true experimental contrast existed at the classroom level. As indicated earlier, during the study, 1 1/2 hours per day were spent on reading in all classrooms for a total of 7 1/2 hours a week. Less time was spent on basal instruction in the experimental rooms, allowing time for the literature component. Generally speaking, E1 and E2 teachers spent about 3 1/2 hours a week with basals and 4 hours with literature. The total 7 1/2 hours a week was given to basal instruction in the control group, allowing for extra time for skill development.

It was not possible nor would it have been ethical to restrict storybook reading entirely in control classes. Control teachers, if they chose, could read stories to their classes, but no more often than twice a week. They were, however, given no instruction on story reading strategies nor did the teachers perceive this as a part of their reading instructional program. Control rooms were observed once a week during reading instruction to record the nature of their instruction and to be sure that they weren't including treatment used in the experimental group.

4 Collection and Analysis of the Quantitative Data Measurements

A number of different measurements were administered during the study, some individually and some in groups. Measures for quantitative experimental data fell into two categories: literacy achievement and use of literature.

Literacy Achievement

Instruments used to evaluate growth in comprehension, writing, and language included standardized group, informal group, and individualized pre- and post-tests. A description of each test follows.

Tests used to evaluate comprehension—more specifically, literal, inferential, and critical comprehension, plus sense of story structure and ability to sequence stories—made use of children's storybooks. Different books, of course, were chosen for use in pre- and post-testing respectively. Specific storybooks were chosen for use in testing in full awareness of the fact that story preferences are often individual and idiosyncratic (Monson & Sebesta, 1991). However, books were chosen for testing purposes in the present study primarily because of the strong quality of their plot structures, including strongly delineated characters, definite settings, clear themes, obvious plot episodes, and definite resolutions. Each story is similar in number of pages and words. All involve concepts and kinds of characters that have been reported as familiar and interesting to second grade children.

Because a major purpose of the study was to determine if a literature-based program could improve comprehension among children of diverse backgrounds, some of the books were selected intentionally to include characters from diverse backgrounds—*Jenny Learns a Lesson* (Fujikawa, 1980), for example, which pictures white, black, Asian, and Hispanic children. Such diversity in character and setting would likely ensure that the diverse population of subjects in the study could relate to the stories. Other books were chosen that had animals for their main characters, again because they were likely to favor no one ethnic or cultural group. Finally, books were also chosen for testing if they were likely to be among those most accessible and most likely to be encountered in a typical American elementary school. All of the books had been used in previous studies with other children from diverse backgrounds (Morrow & Smith, 1988; Morrow, O'Connor, & Smith, 1990). Specific pre- and post-testing books for the oral and written retellings are listed in the appendix.

Story retelling and rewriting is a holistic measure of comprehension which demonstrates not only retention of facts, but also the ability to construct meaning by relating parts of a text to one another. For purposes of the present study, research assistants administered retelling tests on an individual basis; classroom teachers, on the other hand, administered rewriting tests to whole groups. All who administered tests were trained in such testing techniques.

Retelling and Rewriting Tests (Morrow, 1985) were used to analyze literal knowledge of stories, specific elements of story structure, and story sequencing. Children listened to a story that was read to them, then were asked to retell it or rewrite it as if they were telling it to a friend who had never heard it before. No prompts were given with the rewriting test. In tape-recorded oral retelling tests, prompts were limited to questions that were not specific to the plot of the story at hand, generic prompts such as "Then what happened?" or "What comes next?" Both written and oral retellings were evaluated for the inclusion of story structure elements: setting, theme, plot episodes, and resolution. A child received credit for partial recall or for understanding the "gist" of a story event (Pellegrini & Galda, 1982; Thorndyke, 1977).

Scorers also observed sequence by comparing the order of events in the child's retelling with that in the original, determining the ability to make relationships between story elements and to construct a meaningful presentation. Reliability and validity were based on prior use of the instrument with children from diverse backgrounds (Morrow, 1985; Morrow & Smith, 1988; Morrow, O'Connor, & Smith, 1990). In evaluating both retelling and rewriting, reliability was in the range of 90 percent and above. In addition, comparison of the ratings of eight coders for five subjects in this study yielded agreements among the coders of 95 percent for story retelling and 96 percent for story rewriting. The appendix lists specific books used in pre- and post-testing for oral and written retelling.

A Probed Recall Comprehension Test was administered by a research assistant to each child after he or she had read the story. Research assistants had been trained beforehand to administer the test (Morrow, 1985). The test included eight traditional comprehension questions that focused on detail, cause and effect, classifying, inference, and critical judgments, plus eight questions that focused on story structure: setting, theme, plot episodes, and resolution. Research assistants read the questions and recorded the children's answers on test forms. Reliability and validity were based on prior use of this instrument with children from diverse backgrounds (Morrow & Smith, 1988; Morrow, O'Connor, & Smith, 1990). Reliabilities were in the range of 90 percent and above. In addition, eight different coders for five different subjects in this study yielded a 93 percent agreement for the Probed Recall Comprehension Test. The appendix lists specific books used in the pre- and post-testing.

Oral and Written Creation of Original Stories offered still other measures of literacy achievement in the study. Research assistants had been trained to test each student's oral creation of original stories through his or her tape-recorded dictation of such a story. Classroom teachers had been trained to test written creation of original stories. Dictation was elicited in the following manner: Children were shown five figures—a boy, a rabbit, an elf, a house, and an airplane—and told they could use all or some of the figures to help them create their own stories. A similar procedure was followed in eliciting written stories, but with a different set of figures: a person, an animal, a fantasy character, a home, and a means of transportation. If children stopped during oral presentations, they were asked if they had anything more to add. No prompts were allowed in the written tests.

Whether oral or written, students' original stories were evaluated for sense of story structure evidenced by inclusion of setting, theme, plot episodes, and resolution. Sequence was evaluated by observing whether these elements appeared in the order stated above, which also determined the ability to make relationships between story events and to construct meaningful presentations. Reliability and validity were based on prior use of the instrument with children from diverse backgrounds (Morrow & Smith, 1988; Morrow, O'Connor, & Smith, 1990).

Reliabilities in evaluating both oral and written original pieces were in the high 80 percent and above range. In addition, eight different coders for five different subjects in this study yielded 88 percent agreement for the oral original story and a 90 percent for the written.

The California Test of Basic Skills, a standardized instrument, had been administered by the district in April of the year before the study began and was again administered in April of the year in which the study was completed. Results used for the present investigation were taken from the results of language and reading subtests in those two evaluations.

A *Test of Language Development: Vocabulary and Syntactic Complexity* was used to analyze samples taken from the students' retellings, rewritings, and oral and written creation of original stories. The total number of different words used served as the criterion for vocabulary development, and the average number of words per T-unit as the measure for syntactic complexity. In developmental studies of oral language (Hunt, 1965; O'Donnell, Griffin, & Norris, 1967), researchers have found the T-unit to be a reliable measure of language complexity.

Use of Literature

To determine the amount and type of free reading in and out of school, measures 1, 2, and 3 (described below) were used in experimental and control rooms; measure 4 was used only in experimental classes:

1. Children filled out survey forms concerning their after-school activities on the previous day (Greaney, 1980). Such surveys were completed once before the study began and again at its end. Items referring to voluntary reading were embedded within the lists of activities. The survey asked children to check all the things they did after school and before they ate their dinner, offering them the following choices: (a) played outside, (b) watched TV, (c) read or looked at a book, (d) read or looked at a magazine, (e) played with toys or games, (f) did homework, (g) went to an after-school activity (sports, lessons), (h) went somewhere with a grown-up, (i) listened to records or tapes, (j) did some arts and crafts. Children were asked to complete the same list indicating how they spent their time after dinner until they went to sleep. After check-

ing off each list, they were asked to go back and circle the one thing that they most liked to do.

2. Parents were surveyed about their children's after-school activities and about the literary characteristics of their home environments. Items referring to voluntary reading were embedded in the questions. The following information was solicited in the questionnaire: (a) how often children chose to look at books per week, (b) how many hours children engaged in viewing television, (c) how often children visited the library and if they had library cards, (d) how often children were read to by an adult, (e) whether children's books were present in the home and, if so, how many, and (f) what types of books their children enjoyed reading or looking at.

3. Children were asked to name favorite book titles, authors, and illustrators as indicators of their use of literature.

4. Children kept records of books they read during independent reading and writing periods, plus titles of books checked out from classroom libraries to read at home.

Results of the Quantitative Data

Since individual children could not be randomly assigned to conditions, intact classrooms were used as the unit of analysis in the study, with the classroom mean used in all measures. This procedure was followed also because the behaviors of subjects during independent reading and writing periods were likely to be interdependent. Such interdependence would violate the assumption of independence of experimental units that underlies conventional analysis, that is, analysis with the individual child as basic unit. Three conditions were established within the study: two experimental groups (E1, home- and school-based program; and E2, school-based-only program), and one control group. As indicated earlier, each group included three classrooms of children. Data were analyzed through a one-way, repeated-measures analysis of covariance. In the analysis, the pretests served as a covariate and the post-tests were the dependent measure. Post-hoc comparisons were carried out for each analysis using Bonferroni's ad-

justment on the least-square estimate of means to determine which be-
tween-group differences were significant. On all measures, the tests for
homogeneity of the within-group regressions, an assumption of the
analysis of covariance (Winer, 1971), were nonsignificant.

Literacy Achievement

Comprehension Tests

The first three dependent variables in the study consisted of scores on
the free recall Story Retelling Test, the free recall Story Rewriting
Test, and the Probed Recall Comprehension Test. Data were analyzed
separately for each test and for the subcategories within each test using
ANCOVA.

Table 1 presents the pre- and post-test means and standard deviations for the Story Retelling Test. The ANCOVA for the total score on
the retelling measure, $F (2,5) = 12.11$, $p < .01$, showed that the experimental group scored significantly better than the control. Post-hoc
comparisons revealed that both experimental groups, E1 and E2, were
different from the control group but not different from each other.

Table 1 also presents the pre- and post-test means and standard deviations for the Story Rewriting Test. The ANCOVA for the total score on
the rewriting measure, $F (2,5) = 10.71$, $p < .006$, showed that the experimental group scored significantly better than the control. Post-hoc
comparisons revealed that both experimental groups, E1 and E2, were
different from the control group; however, they were not different from
each other.

The pre- and post-test means and standard deviations for the Probed
Recall Comprehension Test are also found on Table 1. The ANCOVA
for the total score on this test, $F (2,5)$ 9.24, $p < .03$, showed that the experimental group scored significantly better than the control. Post-hoc
comparisons revealed that both experimental groups scored significantly better than the control group, but they were not different from
each other.

Creating Original Stories

An ANCOVA compared the post-test performances of the three groups
on creating original oral and original written stories. Table 1 presents
the pre- and post-test means and standard deviations for the creation of

Table 1

Means and Standard Deviations for Literacy Achievement Measures

| | Group* | | | | | | | | | | | |
| | Experimental 1 | | | | Experimental 2 | | | | Control | | | |
	Pretest	(SD)	Post-test	(SD)	Pretest	(SD)	Post-test	(SD)	Pretest	(SD)	Post-test	(SD)
Story Retelling	4.07	(1.40)	7.39^a	(2.40)	3.88	(.62)	6.80^a	(2.12)	4.87	(2.14)	4.72^b	(1.40)
Story Rewriting	3.63	(1.68)	8.01^a	(2.14)	4.37	(2.31)	7.11^a	(3.21)	4.60	(2.10)	4.59^b	(2.14)
Probed Comprehension	15.70	(3.02)	23.13^a	(3.95)	14.74	(3.12)	21.22^a	(3.60)	15.08	(3.15)	14.59^b	(3.60)
Oral Original Stories	6.18	(2.42)	12.86^a	(3.01)	5.28	(1.81)	11.11^a	(3.21)	4.70	(1.61)	3.27^b	(1.71)
Written Original Stories	6.18	(2.10)	10.94^a	(2.42)	6.01	(1.62)	9.02^a	(3.61)	5.58	(1.41)	5.23^b	(2.11)
California Test of Basic Skills Reading	58.47	(4.16)	62.62^a	(4.26)	60.02	(4.14)	62.61^a	(4.87)	57.62	(5.61)	59.54^b	(5.01)
Language	58.61	(4.66)	62.60^a	(5.09)	67.20	(5.62)	70.26^a	(5.29)	61.53	(5.23)	64.70^a	(5.12)

Note: Post-test means are adjusted for pretest scores

*n = 3 for each group

[a,b,c]Post-test scores are significantly different ($p < .05$) if they do not share the same superscript.

oral original stories. The ANCOVA for the total score on the original story measure, F (2,5) = 9.87, p < .02, showed that the experimental groups scored significantly better than the control. Post-hoc comparisons revealed that both experimental groups scored significantly better than the control, but were not different from each other.

The pre- and post-test means and standard deviations for the original written stories are on Table 1. The ANCOVA for total score on this measure, F (2,5) = 9.70, p < .01, showed that the experimental groups scored significantly better than the control. In post-hoc comparisons, the experimental groups were different from the control group, but not from each other.

California Test of Basic Skills

Table 1 presents the pre- and post-test means and standard deviations for the California Test of Basic Skills. The ANCOVA for the total reading score on this measure, F (2,5) = .02, p < 10, and the language scores, F (2,5) = .74, p < 6, showed no significant differences between the groups.

Language Complexity and Vocabulary Development

Table 2 presents the pre- and post-test means and standard deviations for the language measures in the oral and written story retellings and oral and written dictation of original stories. The number of different words used was the measure of vocabulary development, and length of T-unit was the measure of language complexity. The ANCOVA for the number of different words used in the written story retelling, F (2,5) = 7.47, p < .04, the written original story, F (2,5) = 5.51, p < .05, and the oral original story, F (2,5) = 6.47, p < .05, showed that the experimental groups scored significantly better than the control. Post-hoc comparisons revealed that both E1 and E2 were different from the control group, but not from each other. There were no significant differences in the number of different words used in the oral retellings, F (2,5) = 1.46, p < .36.

The pre- and post-test means and standard deviations for the average length per T-unit appear on Table 2. The ANCOVA indicated that there were significant differences between the groups in the written retellings, F = (2,5) 12.94, p < .01; the written original story, F (2,5) = 9.79, p < .05; and the oral original story, F (2,5) = 4.01, p < .05. Post-hoc

Table 2

Means and Standard Deviations for Language Complexity and Vocabulary Development

| | Group* | | | | | | | | | | | |
| | Experimental 1[1] | | | | Experimental 2[2] | | | | Control[3] | | | |
	Pretest	(SD)	Post-test	(SD)	Pretest	(SD)	Post-test	(SD)	Pretest	(SD)	Post-test	(SD)
Number of Different Words												
Written Story Retelling	56.48	(12.30)	61.43[a]	(12.37)	44.07	(11.27)	55.94[a]	(12.61)	23.64	(10.21)	29.11[b]	(12.43)
Written Original Story	36.20	(11.20)	44.56[a]	(11.10)	41.92	(10.27)	47.17[a]	(10.20)	28.30	(10.26)	27.30[b]	(10.20)
Oral Story Retelling	53.86	(9.89)	74.74[a]	(11.27)	49.46	(10.18)	71.09[a]	(14.23)	60.39	(11.32)	73.34[a]	(11.69)
Oral Original Story	46.97	(10.21)	62.25[a]	(10.61)	42.77	(9.26)	57.46[a]	(12.04)	37.79	(12.17)	41.12[b]	(13.27)
Average T-unit Length												
Written Story Retelling	5.65	(0.20)	6.56[a]	(0.18)	5.74	(0.21)	6.46[a]	(0.22)	5.37	(0.22)	5.31[b]	(0.18)
Written Original Story	6.29	(0.21)	7.12[a]	(0.20)	6.02	(0.11)	6.95[a]	(0.25)	6.13	(0.25)	5.39[b]	(0.20)
Oral Story Retelling	5.87	(0.28)	7.67[a]	(0.25)	5.84	(0.25)	7.18[a]	(0.30)	5.86	(0.20)	7.39[a]	(0.24)
Oral Original Story	6.79	(0.21)	7.17[a]	(0.23)	6.29	(0.21)	6.67[a]	(0.21)	5.87	(0.21)	6.10[b]	(0.28)

Note: Post-test means are adjusted for pretest scores

*n = 3 for each group

[a,b,c]Post-test scores are significantly different ($p < .05$) if they do not share the same superscript.

comparisons showed that in the written retellings and the written original stories, E1 and E2 were different from the control group, but not different from each other. In the original oral story, E1 was different from the control, but E2 was not different from E1 or the control. T-unit length demonstrated no significant differences between any groups on the oral retellings $F (2,5) = .05$, $p < 9$.

Comparison of Scores between African American and White Students

As reported in the method's section, the children in this study were from diverse backgrounds. Because of this diversity, it is important to look at the scores from the individual groups to determine if the improvement took place only in certain groups. It is also important because questions have been raised concerning the effectiveness of the treatment used in this study with minority children. The means, standard deviations, and range of scores for black and white children respectively in the experimental and control groups on nine of the literacy measures were studied to determine if one group was superior to another and thus responsible for the significant gains in the investigation. Because the Hispanic and Asian populations were relatively small (a total of 27 Latino and 9 Asians dispersed among the experimental and control groups), their scores were not reviewed.

The data presented in Tables 3 and 4 demonstrate that pre- and posttest means, standard deviations, and range of scores for the experimental and control groups were extremely similar for the 72 black students (48 in the experimental group and 24 in the control) and 60 white students (39 in the experimental group and 21 in the control); therefore, the presence of neither blacks nor whites could have been responsible for the significant differences in gains for the experimental group or lack of change in the control. Children from all backgrounds in all groups shared equally in the results of the study. Because there were no differences found between the experimental and control groups, scores of the black and white children were not compared on the California Test of Basic Skills.

Use of Literature

Several different measures were used to determine the amount of literature use in and out of school, some with the experimental groups only and some with both experimental and control groups.

Table 3

Means and Standard Deviations, and Range of Literacy Test Scores for Black and White Children in Experimental Groups

	Pretest						Post-test					
	White			Black			White			Black		
Measure	M	(SD)	Range (H–L)	M	(SD)	Range (H–L)	M	(SD)	Range (H–L)	M	(SD)	Range (H–L)
Story Retelling	4.28	(1.50)	7.7–1.7	4.80	(1.20)	6.8–1.7	7.73	(1.50)	7.5– 1.7	7.87	(0.95)	9.9– 4.1
Story Rewriting	5.89	(2.37)	9.5–1.0	4.34	(1.50)	7.5–1.5	8.50	(2.12)	9.5– 2.0	7.29	(1.42)	9.1– 3.4
Probed Comprehension	16.46	(4.50)	20.0–6.0	15.05	(2.96)	18.5–7.0	24.15	(3.00)	28.0–16.0	22.78	(2.87)	26.5–15.0
Oral Original Story	8.70	(3.37)	13.5–1.0	8.46	(3.13)	13.5–1.0	10.70	(2.75)	14.0– 3.0	10.80	(2.25)	14.0– 5.0
Written Original Story	7.14	(2.00)	13.0–5.0	6.61	(2.62)	11.5–1.0	10.80	(1.87)	13.5– 6.0	9.80	(2.00)	14.0– 6.0
T-unit Retelling	6.10	(1.60)	8.1–1.7	5.90	(1.40)	7.6–2.0	7.80	(1.00)	8.1– 4.0	7.80	(0.67)	9.1– 6.4
T-unit Rewriting	5.76	(1.20)	8.4–3.6	5.99	(0.50)	7.0–5.0	8.10	(1.22)	9.2– 4.3	7.77	(1.17)	8.7– 4.0
T-unit Oral Original	7.80	(1.70)	8.7–4.0	7.90	(0.90)	8.6–5.0	7.50	(1.20)	9.8– 5.1	8.60	(0.92)	9.7– 6.0
T-unit Written Original	6.15	(1.00)	8.3–4.0	6.17	(0.70)	8.3–5.5	7.30	(1.00)	9.8– 5.5	7.34	(1.10)	9.7– 5.2

Table 4

Means, Standard Deviations, and Range of Literacy Test Scores for Black and White Children in Control Groups

| | Pretest | | | | | | Post-test | | | | | |
| | White | | | Black | | | White | | | Black | | |
Measure	M	(SD)	Range (H–L)	M	(SD)	Range (H–L)	M	(SD)	Range (H–L)	M	(SD)	Range (H–L)
Story Retelling	4.51	(2.50)	10.9–1.2	4.96	(1.75)	8.6–1.5	4.87	(1.25)	7.8–2.1	5.20	(1.75)	8.8–2.2
Story Rewriting	4.69	(1.50)	7.2–1.0	4.97	(2.00)	8.7–1.2	4.86	(1.00)	5.2–1.1	4.06	(1.20)	7.4–1.8
Probed Comprehension	15.05	(4.50)	23.5–5.0	13.79	(4.00)	19.2–4.1	15.67	(3.10)	21.2–9.2	14.80	(3.10)	22.6–8.5
Oral Original Story	5.31	(3.00)	13.2–2.2	5.41	(2.70)	12.4–1.9	4.38	(1.70)	7.2–1.2	5.91	(1.70)	7.4–2.1
Written Original Story	6.78	(2.70)	11.8–2.4	5.58	(3.00)	12.6–2.2	6.56	(2.40)	11.7–1.2	5.79	(2.10)	10.8–2.1
T-unit Retelling	5.77	(1.20)	7.6–2.1	6.00	(0.75)	7.5–3.1	6.10	(1.30)	8.6–2.1	6.70	(1.60)	9.6–3.3
T-unit Rewriting	5.92	(0.87)	7.5–4.0	5.25	(1.10)	8.5–4.0	5.45	(1.70)	7.2–1.1	5.51	(1.20)	7.8–2.1
T-unit Oral Original	6.43	(1.70)	8.5–2.1	5.35	(1.60)	8.2–1.1	6.50	(2.20)	10.2–2.2	5.80	(1.80)	8.9–1.1
T-unit Written Original	6.24	(0.95)	8.8–5.5	5.51	(0.97)	8.5–4.6	6.81	(1.00)	8.2–4.2	5.90	(0.75)	7.6–4.3

After-School Activities

Children in the experimental and control groups filled out questionnaires asking them to indicate their after-school activities on the previous day (Greaney, 1980). These surveys were completed once at the beginning of the school year and once at the end. Items referring to voluntary reading were embedded among such other activities as "watched TV" or "played with a friend."

Table 5 presents the pre- and post-test means and standard deviations for the reading options on the survey. The ANCOVA for both reading items, "read or looked at a book," $F(2,5) = 4.14$, $p < .01$ and "read or looked at a magazine," $F(2,5) = 3.29$, $p < .02$, showed that the experimental groups scored significantly better than the control. The experimental groups, however, were not different from each other. There were no significant differences in the groups on the item, "was read to by an adult," $F(2,5) = 1.24$, $p < .14$.

Parent Questionnaire

Parents were asked to fill out questionnaires revealing literacy activities in which children engaged at home. Literacy items were embedded in the questionnaire. Because only 50 percent of the questionnaires were returned and most of those represented homes of subjects in the experimental groups, no analysis was done.

Naming Book Titles, Authors, and Illustrators

Literature use was measured through interviews which asked experimental and control children to name their favorite book titles, authors, and illustrators. This was looked upon as a measure of literature use, because it was assumed that a child was more likely to be able to perform this task if he or she were reading books, looking at books, or being exposed to books by the teacher. Table 6 presents the pre- and post-interview results for the total number of books, authors, and illustrators named, as well as total number of different books, authors, and illustrators named by children in the three groups. In all cases, the experimental groups named more book titles, authors, and illustrators than the control group.

Table 5

Means and Standard Deviations for Reading Activities Done After School

Questionnaire Item	Group*											
	Experimental 1				Experimental 2				Control			
	Pretest	(SD)	Post-test	(SD)	Pretest	(SD)	Post-test	(SD)	Pretest	(SD)	Post-test	(SD)
Read a book	12.60	(1.20)	18.40	(3.20)[b]	13.60	(1.20)	20.50	(2.20)[b]	12.10	(2.20)	13.60	(2.30)[b]
Read a magazine	2.80	(1.02)	14.20	(1.20)[b]	3.60	(1.10)	16.20	(1.58)[b]	3.20	(0.98)	5.60	(1.60)[b]
An adult read to me	3.20	(1.12)	4.20	(1.21)[b]	4.20	(1.40)	4.80	(1.20)[b]	4.40	(0.98)	4.60	(1.60)[b]

Note: Post-test means are adjusted for pretest scores.

*n = 3 for all groups

[b,c]Post-test scores are significantly different ($p < .05$) if they do not share the same superscript.

Table 6

Books, Authors, and Illustrators Named

	Experimental 1		Experimental 2		Control	
	Pretest	Post-test	Pretest	Post-test	Pretest	Post-test
# of books	95	137	92	134	96	91
# of different books	77	110	88	108	77	79
# of authors	40	77	30	63	35	40
# of different authors	9	29	8	26	8	13
# of illustrators	0	10	1	9	2	4
# of different illustrators	0	8	1	7	2	4

Books Read in School and Taken Home to Read

Two other sources provided information on children's use of literature. Children in the experimental groups were asked to record on index cards the dates and titles of books they read on their own in school. They also recorded the dates and titles of classroom library books taken home to read. These data were not completely reliable because some children were more efficient about keeping their records than others. The two sets of data were combined and looked at for increased book use over time. (The data were collected for the experimental group only, since the control children did not participate in either activity.)

There were 102 children in the six experimental rooms, 49 boys and 53 girls. We reviewed records of books read in class and those taken home from the beginning of November to the end of April. The time was divided into three periods: November–December, January–February, and March–April. The number of books for each time period was recorded to note if the numbers increased over time. A total of 1,679 books were recorded as read in school or at home, 953 by 53 girls and 726 by 49 boys. Fifteen percent of the books were read in the first time period, 35 percent in the second, and 50 percent in the third. Girls read more books than boys, averaging 17.06 to the boys' average of 14.71.

5 Collection and Analysis of the Qualitative Data

This study showed quantitatively that when compared with a control group, students who participated in the experimental program gained significantly in ability to retell and rewrite stories, in probed-recall comprehension test results, in ability to create oral and written stories, in vocabulary, and in ability to comprehend syntactic complexity.

Qualitative data in the study were collected through (1) interviews reflecting student and teacher attitudes toward "traditional" reading instruction and toward the experimental literature-based program, and (2) in-depth observations documented during periods of independent reading and writing. The purpose of these observations was to determine the types of literacy activities participated in during those periods and the socially interactive behavior that seemed to motivate reading and writing. Analysis of these qualitative data would improve understanding of why the experimental groups tended to score better than the control group in the quantitative analyses described in Chapter 4.

Attitudes Toward the Literature-Based Reading Program

For purposes of this study, attitudes toward the literature-based reading program were solicited only from children and teachers in the experimental groups. It was assumed that those attitudes would be based on comparisons with characteristics of the traditional basal-reading-only program used in the two schools before the experimental study was undertaken. Summaries of students' and teachers' responses to the questions posed are presented here.

Teacher Interviews

Though the six teachers in the experimental groups were interviewed individually, their comments were extremely consistent. In general, they reported initial skepticism about the amount of time that the literature-based program would take away from other classroom activities (such as basal reading instruction), but their feelings changed over time. By the end of the study, they saw literature as an integral part of their reading instruction program. All reported initial concerns about getting children to work on-task during LCT, but they were able over time to work those problems through. They also generally agreed in their plans to continue working with a literature-based program and to further integrate literature with their basal instruction.

Certain categories of general agreement emerged in the teachers' responses to interview questions. The categories are listed below with bullets. Each is then followed by more specific responses which led to creating the categories.

What did your children like about the literature-based program?

- Children like choices and self-directed activities such as
  whether to read or write alone or with others.
  whether or not to use story manipulatives such as feltboards and taped stories alone or with others.

- Children like teacher-modeled literature activities such as
  being read to by the teacher.
  the teacher's chalk talks and other forms of storytelling.

- Children like a prepared literacy environment such as
  the literacy center and its elements of comfort such as the rocking chair, rug, pillows, and stuffed animals.

What did the children learn from participating in the program?

- Children learned many skills, for example
  vocabulary and comprehension were enhanced.
  sense of story structure was improved.
  skills stressed in basals were reinforced.
  knowledge about authors and illustrators was increased.

- Children developed positive attitudes toward reading.
  Children expressed the fact that they like reading.
  Children participated in LCTs voluntarily and with enthusiasm.

- Children learned to interact socially.
  Children cooperated when participating in literature-based activities.
  Children helped each other and engaged in peer tutoring.

What did you learn from participating in the literature program?

- Choice was a factor that motivated literacy activity.
  Choice provided literacy activity for advanced children, slow children, and those with special needs.
  Children chose activities that were meaningful to them. They wrote about current events that occurred during the study, and about television programs, rock stars, and real-life experiences.

- It is important to provide children with LCTs because
  the "social family" atmosphere encouraged reading and writing.
  LCTs encouraged cooperation, enabling children to learn from each other.

- The importance of facilitating and modeling literacy activity:
  Facilitating learning by interacting with children during LCTs was as important as directly teaching skills.
  Modeling literacy behaviors was as important as direct teaching.

- Insights gained about basal and literature-based instruction:
  The basal organized word recognition skill development.
  The literature-based program emphasized vocabulary and comprehension.
  The programs complemented each other and should be used simultaneously.

Child Interviews

To determine their attitudes toward reading and the literature program, the ninety-two children in the experimental groups were interviewed individually and asked the questions reported below. As indicated above, only children in the experimental groups were interviewed, since children in the control group would not have been able to answer questions concerning attitudes toward the literature-based program nor to compare it with basal-only instruction. As with teacher interviews, categories emerged from students' responses to the interview questions. Those categories are listed with bullets, each followed by more specific responses that clustered into that category. Finally, the number of children who made such a response or one very similar to it is recorded in parenthesis, e.g., (n=32).

What do you learn in the literature program?

- Skill development:
  You learn to read better because you read a lot. (n=85)
  You learn to understand what you are reading. (n=55)
  You learn a lot of new words. (n=60)
  You learn that authors and illustrators are real people like yourself. (n=30)
  You learn how to read better because kids who are good readers help you. (n=25)

- Positive attitudes toward reading and writing:
  You learn that reading can make you feel happy. (n=82)
  You learn that writing can be fun. (n=50)

What do you learn in your regular reading groups?

- Skill development:
  You learn to read stories in a book the teacher gives to you. (n=48)
  You learn how to spell and sound out hard words. (n=41)
  You learn to answer questions and memorize. (n=42)
  You do worksheets to learn vowels and accents. (n=42)
  You learn to pay attention and to raise your hand. (n=26)

What do you do and like to do in the literature program?

- Literacy activities children like to do:
  I get to read a lot. (n=88)
  I can write stories. (n=34)
  I tell felt stories, tape stories, and chalk talks. (n=82)

- Use of the classroom environment during the literature program:
  I like the Book Nook. It's cozy. It's a special place.
  You can read on the carpet, in the rocking chair, or leaning on pillows. (n=61)
  I would like the Book Nook to have more books, and I'd like to be able to use it on more days. (n=35)
  The only thing the Book Nook needs to make it better is food, like a snack bar. (n=10)

- Social atmosphere and choices in the program:
  You can choose what you want to read, like reading long books, short books, hard books, or easy books. (n=75)

I like to work with my friends on reading and writing things. (n=52)

- Positive attitudes toward activities in the literature program:
  There are lots of good books that I like to read. (n=51)
  When I read here it makes me feel happy. (n=88)
  The felt stories, taped stories and other things are fun. (n=62)

What do you do and like to do in regular reading?

- Literacy activities children do during regular reading:
  You get only one fat long book to read that's boring. (n=51)
  We do mostly workbook pages. (n=32)
  You take tests, answer questions, and be quiet. (n=20)
  During regular reading you work; during LCT you read. (n=25)

- Use of the classroom environment during regular reading:
  You must sit in your seat when you work. (n=25)

- Lack of choices during regular reading:
  You can't choose what you read. The teacher tells you what to read and it is the same for everyone. (n=35)
  You have to read stories again when you don't read well, and the class gets ahead of you and you feel bad. (n=10)

Do the teachers act the same in regular reading and during the literature program?

- Teacher as director and facilitator:
  In regular reading the teacher says, "You have to read this now." In the literature program she lets you choose what you want to read or write. (n=22)
  In the literature program the teacher reads to you and with you. She never does that in regular reading. (n=18)
  During regular reading the teacher is bossy. She talks to everyone at once and doesn't help very much. During recreational reading she talks to everyone by themselves, helps us, and does stuff with us like a friend. (n=48)

Observational Data

The six second grade classrooms in which the treatment occurred were observed as a formal part of the study. Observational data were collected in three ways. First, six research assistants observed and re-corded field notes for 30-minute independent reading and writing peri-ods once a week in each classroom from October through May, a total of 175 observations over 85 hours, during which 714 episodes were re-corded. Second, once a month, activities within a 30-minute LCT in each of the six rooms were videotaped, a total of 24 hours. Finally, children and teachers were interviewed on their perceptions of the pro-gram and its three major components: literacy centers in classrooms, literature-based instruction, and LCTs. Triangulation through the use of these several different approaches to data collection, field notes, transcribed videotapes, and interviews provided interrelated data from several different perspectives, as well as the ability to compare data at two or more different points in time.

Data collection proceeded through three phases (Corsaro, 1985; Lin-coln & Guba, 1985). In the first month, observers familiarized them-selves with the children and the teachers, and established their role as individuals collecting field notes or videotaping in the classroom. The first sets of field notes and videotapes were based on instructional guidesheets prepared for the research assistants. This first phase not only provided an initial data source for evaluating data quality and vid-eos, but also allowed the refining and standardization of procedures to assure that the kinds of data sought were actually being collected. The second phase involved the collection of data based on those refined pro-cedures for field notes and videotaping. The third phase was devoted to interviewing the teachers and children who participated.

Developed by the investigators, the guidesheets for research assis-tants included instructions on how to observe in an educational setting as well as how to focus on the behaviors of children and teachers during LCT. Two kinds of observation were anticipated. The more typical cov-ered complete interaction episodes, that is, they described events that occurred during LCT and documented them using notes and video-tapes. Episodes were expected to thoroughly depict such issues as how students selected activities, how they interacted socially, and what learning of literacy took place. Complete interaction episodes were to be followed from beginning to end and to include dialogue. Data on in-teraction were to include group or personal goals, support given by group members to other group members, time on task, types of partici-pation by different group members (i.e., leaders, followers), materials used, names of children, gender, and proxemics or body movement, and use of space (Bogdan & Biklen, 1982; Fetterman, 1984; Green & Wallat, 1981). This type of note taking and videotaping is referred to by Barker (1963) as the stream-of-behavior chronicle in which minute-by-minute accounts are recorded about what subjects do and say.

Episode records also noted teacher behavior, including how they interacted with youngsters, specific roles they played (e.g., participant, facilitator, instructor) and the nature of their dialogue (e.g., supportive, controlling, evaluative). At least two teacher episodes were to be recorded during each observation.

In addition to recording episodes, at least four times each half hour, each observer was to conduct a "scan" to record the array of simultaneous activity under way at a given moment, including the general atmosphere in the classroom, the kinds of activity occurring, movement, noise, and the like.

Interviews were conducted one-on-one with teachers and children. While different interview outlines and questions were prepared for teachers and children, all were composed of open-ended questions prepared in advance and providing a framework within which respondents could express their understanding of the situation in their own terms (Patton, 1990).

Investigators and research assistants met weekly during the first three weeks of data collection, sharing notes and observations, viewing videotapes, and discussing transcriptions to determine if the data being collected were consistent among observers in type and amount, and to assure that the data collected were actually focusing on the questions being investigated. After the first three meetings, bimonthly meetings continued in order to further clarify and standardize data collection procedures (Morrow, Sharkey, & Firestone, 1993).

Data Analysis

Our approach to data analysis was not strictly inductive, since we began with a strong theoretical base that stemmed from previous research and that had led to the development of the program being studied (Morrow, O'Connor, & Smith, 1990; Morrow, 1992). Nor was it strictly deductive since we wanted to discover and elaborate those processes that might link the physical and social aspects of the program with its outcomes as well as expand the range of outcomes considered (Rossman & Wilson, 1985). Adapting a research procedure used by Miles and Huberman (1984), we viewed the processes of data collection, data reduction, data display, and the drawing and verifying of conclusions as interactively interwoven, each feeding the other. For example, meetings of research assistants and investigators initially focused primarily on data collection, but later included data analysis, as well as discussion of the broad categories and subcategories that emerged as observations continued. These discussions refined and clarified the definitions of various analytic categories.

Periods of formal analysis alternated between macroanalysis intended to identify broad patterns, and microanalysis in which the frequency of specific categories was assessed (Alvermann, O'Brien, & Dillon, 1990). Both required frequent reading and rereading of field notes and transcripts as well as viewing of videotapes. Macroanalysis further clarified the meaning of categories, identified their significance for literacy learning, and described and elucidated processes at work in the classroom. Microanalysis focused more specifically and rigorously on developing frequencies and percentages.

Episodes were coded by analytic categories. Episodes that could be placed in more than one category were coded into all in which they were appropriate. To determine overall frequency, the number of incidents within each category and subcategory was first totaled. Then the number of incidents in each subcategory was divided by the number of incidents within its main category, yielding a percentage.

To determine reliability in the coding and categorizing of incidents, five third-party individuals were asked to code the same six recorded observations of an LCT. Each observation came from a different classroom representing one or another of the several teachers participating in the study. The five coders were told the purpose of the study and given definitions of the categories and subcategories. They were shown how to categorize the incidents, then given the raw data to analyze. The reliability check indicated a high percentage of agreement among them, ranging from 85 to 90 percent across all categories and subcategories (Morrow, Sharkey, & Firestone, 1993).

Results of the Data Analysis

An independent reading and writing period in a classroom literacy center as reported here is characterized by a great variety of behavior. Children are engaged actively and cooperatively. They take turns, change roles, offer information, and make decisions as they engage in literacy activity, as the following scan of one classroom illustrates:

> Several children were curled up on the rug, leaning on pillows in the literacy center with books they had selected to read silently. Damien and Larry squeezed tightly into one rocking chair, sharing a book.
>
> Natalie, Shakiera, and Dharmesh were snuggled in a large refrigerator box that had been painted to make it more attractive. Furnished with stuffed animals to make it look cozier, it created a "private spot" for reading. They took turns reading the same book.
>
> Isabela and Veronica were using the feltboard and story characters for *The Three Bears* (Galdone, 1975), taking turns reading and manipulating the figures. When they came to repetitive phrases such as, "Who's been sitting in my chair?" they read them together.
>
> Four children were listening on headsets to a tape of *The Little Engine that Could* (Piper, 1954). Each child held a copy of the book and chanted along with the narrator every time they came to the phrase "I think I can, I think I can."
>
> Matthew and Gabriel were at the author's table writing an informational book about snakes, bouncing ideas back and forth. Several children were checking books out of the classroom library to take home to read, signing a form on a clipboard.
>
> Tashiba had multiple copies of a story that she handed out to other children. She made a circle of chairs where the group then sat as she pretended to be the teacher. She read to the others, occasionally stopping to ask if anyone else wanted a chance to read. Mrs. Bell, their teacher, sat in the circle with the children, taking her turn at reading when Tashiba called on her.

There is a pattern in this diverse activity. Figure 1 illustrates that pattern and shows how the physical and social contexts led to two analytically distinct, but interrelated processes: literacy behavior and social interaction. These, in turn, contributed to a wide range of positive outcomes. Because we have already described those contexts, we now

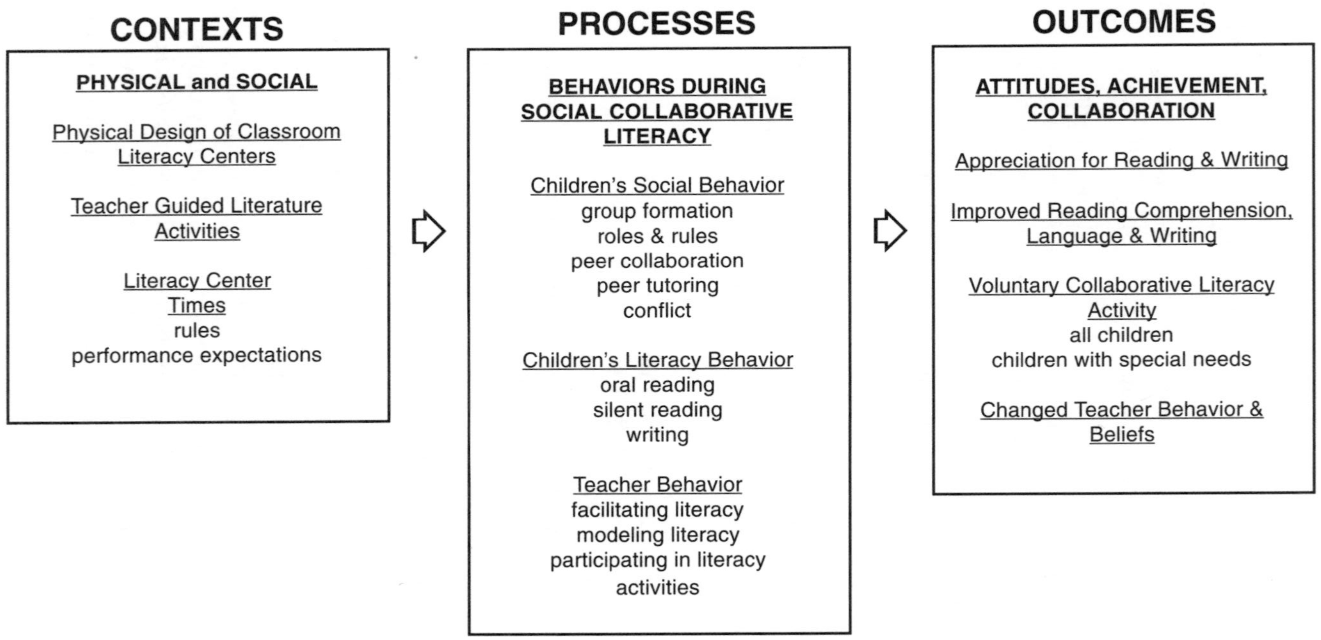

Figure 1. Contexts, Processes, and Outcomes Fostered by Collaborative Literacy Settings.

focus on the processes (including the social and literacy activities of student and teacher participants) and the outcomes that result.

Processes during Independent Reading and Writing Periods

Social Processes

The scan presented earlier implies correctly that collaborative incidents were constant and predominant during LCT. As reported in the literature review, collaboration in small groups promotes both achievement and productivity (Johnson, et al., 1981; Slavin, 1983). Johnson, et al. (1981) note that both oral interaction among students and heterogeneity among group members contribute to cooperative learning. They also found that learners with special needs benefit from the dialogue and interaction that occurs in small groups, and suggest that higher levels of learning are achieved because children explain material to each other, listen to each others' explanations, and arrive at joint understandings.

Properly planned and implemented, the LCT encourages students to form groups and to develop their own rules and leadership patterns. Group settings, in turn, provide for and accommodate peer collaboration, peer tutoring, conflict resolution, and nontraditional patterns of teacher-student interaction. Among the 714 incidents recorded in field notes, 318 included episodes of group behavior among students.

How Groups Formed. As noted earlier, during an LCT children could choose to work alone or with others. If they chose to work with others, they could decide who those other individuals were to be. Before joining a group, they could identify the task at hand and the nature of the group simply by asking what was happening or by observing before they decided whether or not to join. The following anecdote illustrates the process.

> Tiffany, Shawni and Carla decided to read "scary" stories in the coat closet, where it was dark. The girls snuggled together and began to read. James stood nearby and watched for a short time. Understanding the nature of the group's activity through his observation, he asked to join them, and the girls agreed that he could.
>
> Tiffany, designated the reader by the group, continued to read. Patrick observed their activity and asked if he could join. He, too,

was admitted. Gabriel stopped by, but apparently decided that the activity wasn't for him and left to find something else to do.

It has been noted that self-selected group formation is often based on personal characteristics (Green & Wallat, 1981). A crucial characteristic in the classrooms observed was gender. Both boys and girls purposely formed single-gender groups, though groups of mixed gender formed as well. In fact, in light of past research indicating that children tend to form single-gender groups (LaFreniere, Strayer, & Gauthier, 1984), the fact that 41 percent of the 318 groups formed in the present study combined genders is significant.

Single-gender groups frequently carried out activities that seem stereotypical of the gender they represented. The activity of mixed-gender groups, on the other hand, tended not to illustrate sex stereotypes, as the following examples of an all-girl, an all-boy, and a mixed group indicate.

> Kimberly and Antoinette looked at a cookbook together, reviewing recipes and making comments.
>
> Kimberly pointed to the index and said, "Look, Antoinette, here they got somethin with marshmallows. Let's look at it."
>
> Antoinette said, "Wow, it's fruit salad with marshmallows! That looks good. I love fruit and marshmallows."
>
> Eric, Damien, Alex, and Danny worked on a roll movie for the story *Kick, Pass, and Run* (Kessler, 1966).
>
> Danny said, "Hey, you guys! Eric and Damien, you draw the football field. I'll do the stands and the goal post with Danny."
>
> Eric asked if he could help with the goal post, but Danny said no, that would be too many drawing the goal post. He suggested instead that Eric draw the people in the stands.
>
> Mary, Tina, Jason, and Kevin were writing an original story and creating cutout figures to use on the feltboard for presentation to the class. When they finished, they decided to tape the story. The group designated Mary as the reader, and Tina and Jason read silently as they followed along with her. Kevin followed the story and placed the cutout characters on the feltboard as they were mentioned. Tina and Jason made sound effects as needed for the story. After the taping, they played it back, listened, and giggled.

Groups ranged in size from two to five members, with two being most common. More than five members seemed to make a group less efficient and to increase the number of conflicts. Frequently, individual children left groups voluntarily when group membership surpassed five. Girls tended most often to form groups of two, while all-boy and mixed-gender groups were often composed of three or more.

Counts to determine the composition of groups overall indicated that 80 percent were cross-race, cross-cultural, or inclusive of children with differing abilities. It appears that most formation of groups was based on interest and friendship.

Although working cooperatively in groups was very common, many children also chose to work alone. They usually read silently, but some also told feltboard or chalk-talk stories by themselves. Equal numbers of boys and girls chose to work alone.

Rules and Leadership Roles. When groups formed, they quickly established their own rules and leadership roles. Commonly, rules involved defining work to be accomplished, assigning responsibilities for that work, and determining the acceptable quality of work. For example:

> Tesha and Cassandra decided to work together with a feltboard version of *The Gingerbread Boy* (Galdone, 1975). They decided to work on the floor. Cassandra told Tesha to carry the book and the cutout characters and she would bring the feltboard.
>
> Tesha said, "We gotta work together to do this, and we gotta hurry to finish 'cause we don't have much time."
>
> Cassandra said, "You read first and I'll put up the cutouts. When we're half done with the story, then I'll read and you put up the pieces."
>
> They began the activity and halfway through the story, they switched roles. Each time they came to the rhyme, "Run, run as fast as you can. You can't catch me, I'm the Gingerbread man!" they read together, laughing and saying what fun they were having.

Leaders who emerged within groups were usually respected by other members of the group:

> Ryan, Alex, and Gabe worked on illustrations for a story they wrote called *The Golden Sword.* They spread out a large picture of a castle and Ryan began to outline it in black marker.
>
> *Ryan:* Alex, go get a black marker and help me outline this.
>
> *Gabe:* Where should I start?
>
> *Ryan:* Right over here. (Alex returned with the marker.)
>
> *Ryan:* Alex, go get a red crayon.

Alex: Why, Ryan?

Ryan: Because we forgot to color this.

Alex: Is a red pencil okay?

Ryan: I guess so. But, Alex, we need a blue crayon too.

Alex: What do we need it for?

Ryan: We forgot to color in the water over here.

Gabe: What color should I do the sky?

Ryan: Blue will look good.

Formation of group rules and emergence of leaders were observed in 175, or 55 percent, of the 318 group incidents recorded.

Collaboration within Groups. When groups formed, children generally collaborated by helping each other carry out literacy projects, by taking turns, sharing materials, and offering information. For example: Rachel and Tashiba decided to use a feltboard together.

> Rachel said, "I want to do this one, *The Tortoise and the Hare*" (Stevens, 1971).
>
> Tashiba said, "Let's do this one, *Rumpelstiltskin*" (Stobbs, 1970).
>
> "I know," said Rachel, "we'll do both."
>
> They decided to do *Rumpelstiltskin* first. Namita and Chabela joined them, but sat silently and listened while Rachel read the story and Tashiba manipulated the cutouts on the feltboard. At the end of the story, Namita asked if she and Chabela could read to Rachel and Tashiba. Everyone seemed pleased as Namita read, Chabela manipulated the figures, and Rachel and Tashiba listened.

Of the 318 groups observed, collaboration was identified in 291 incidents, or 92 percent.

Peer Tutoring. Peer tutoring occurred in at least 66, or 20 percent, of the 318 group episodes recorded. Much of the tutoring was not recorded because children often whispered words and hints to help each other so considerately that they were inaudible to observers and not picked up on videotape.

For the purposes of this study and by definition, peer tutoring is distinguished from peer collaboration because it typically involves one child in a teaching role, offering guidance and assistance to another child. Collaboration, by contrast, tends to find students offering equal amounts of help to each other. As informal peer tutors, children in the 66 identified groups assisted each other in reading words, spelling, and making decisions for the completion of literacy projects. Children sought each other's opinions, as well, and offered positive reinforcement to other group members. The following episode illustrates the variety of peer tutoring activity:

> Jason and Tiffany were in a cozy area of the library corner, each holding a stuffed tiger. Although both children were regularly assigned to basic-skills classrooms, in the present situation Tiffany assumed the role of traditional teacher to help Jason who had started looking through a book of nursery rhymes.
>
> "Let's read this one," Tiffany said. Jason agreed, and Tiffany told him to begin reading.
>
> "I forgot the first word. What does H-E-Y say?"
>
> "That says, 'Hey diddle diddle,'" said Tiffany. "Now you read."
>
> Jason continued, "The cat and the . . . ."
>
> He paused, and Tiffany said, "Look at the letter, it's an F - *ffff.* It says the *fiddle.*"
>
> "Oh," said Jason, ". . . the fiddle, The cow jumped over the moon. Let's do another one."
>
> Tiffany said, "OK." They turned the page and Jason began to read, "Little Betty Blue lost her shoe."
>
> "Wait," Tiffany said, "You gotta read the title first."

Conflicts. Although collaboration was evident within most groups, conflicts did occur in 21 (6 percent) of the 318 recorded episodes. Some involved getting the group organized so that it would function well. Such conflicts often arose in discussions of what activity or book to select. Other conflicts concerned sharing materials and taking turns. Still others dealt directly with carrying out literacy activities. Most conflicts arose naturally and understandably, especially since most of the children participating had not been accustomed to working in such settings nor to making many of their own decisions about what to do and with whom to do it. In spite of that fact, most conflicts were easily resolved.

According to Piaget (1959), learning occurs when a conflict arises and those involved figure out how to settle it. The following anecdote describes a typical conflict and how it was resolved. Tasha and Tamika decided to write a story together about a king and a queen.

> Tasha said, "We have to begin with 'Once upon a time the king and queen lived in a castle.'" She wrote the sentence, but spelled *castle,* K-A-S-A-L.

"You spelled castle wrong," said Tamika. "It's C-A-S-T-L-E, not K-A-S-A-L."

Tasha responded, "Mine sounds right and yours don't."

"Yours does look right," said Tamika, "but spelling is weird sometimes, and I'm right."

"I'll get the dictionary and prove you're wrong," said Tasha.

She looked under "K" for castle and couldn't find it, so reluctantly she looked under "C" and found castle as Tamika had spelled it.

"Okay," you're right. But it still don't look right."

Children themselves resolved 90 percent of the conflicts recorded; in the other 10 percent, either the groups involved disbanded, or the teacher intervened.

Literacy Behavior

Most of the specific literacy activities that took place during independent reading and writing periods were dynamic, manipulative, and quite different from those traditional to basal reading instruction. They fell into three broad categories: oral reading, silent reading, and writing.

Oral reading. Oral reading provides practice with pronunciation, intonation, pacing, and performance, and it can be used to evaluate and analyze reading performance. As a general component of activity, it was common during LCT: all 714 recorded episodes involved some type of literacy behavior, but oral reading occurred in 57 percent of them. Children read aloud to themselves and to each other in pairs and small groups. They shared books, magazines, and newspapers as the following episode illustrates:

Larry grabbed the book *The Magic School Bus Lost in the Solar System* (Cole, 1990) from a bookshelf in the library corner.

"I gotta read this book again," he said to Larry. "It's neat."

The boys sat down on the carpet and Shon, who was standing close by, asked if he could read, too, and they agreed. Larry began reading, then Bryan took a turn and so did Shon. They listened attentively to each other and when they finished, they chose another book to read together.

Opportunity for oral reading is limited in traditional classroom settings and often is tedious for those who are listening. In an LCT, by contrast, children willingly participate in oral reading without being asked. Coercing children to read unchosen materials orally in front of an entire class, typical in traditional settings, can be unpleasant and threatening. During LCT, on the other hand, children often choose to read orally and others choose to listen, for in the context of an LCT, oral reading is productive and pleasant.

Silent Reading. There is a relationship between the amount of time spent reading and achievement in reading (Anderson, Wilson, & Fielding, 1988; Greaney & Hegarty, 1987; Morrow, 1993; Taylor, Frye, & Maruyama, 1990). For two decades and longer, various schools have instituted periods of sustained silent reading to give children the opportunity to read. Laudable as the goal is, such periods tend to be somewhat contrived, since everyone is expected to do the same thing at the same time. By contrast, an LCT gives individuals the opportunity to read silently to themselves, but the opportunity is offered as one of a variety of options.

Silent reading was apparent in 56 percent of the episodes observed and recorded during this study. Children read silently alone or with others nearby or next to them. They curled up on rugs or leaned against pillows or each other, often holding stuffed animals as they read. They read at their desks, in closets, and under desks and tables. One child read silently while walking slowly around the classroom. The following incident is typical of the silent reading observed during the program.

> Five children were reading silently as a group in the literacy center. Leaning on a pillow, Tim read a magazine. Paul leaned against him to read from the same magazine. Mercedes sat in a rocking chair, reading *Bringing the Rain to Kapiti Plain* (Aardema, 1989), and Kelly and Stephanie were under a shelf reading from two different copies of the same book.

In interviews, both children and teachers said that the reading they did during LCT—including both oral and silent reading—improved their ability as readers and writers since they were reading so much. Children also noted that during LCT, help was readily available from peers as well as the teacher, and that taking advantage of that fact helped them improve in reading.

Writing. When given their own choice of topic, according to Graves (1975), children write more often and write longer pieces than when not given their choice. Indeed, children apparently write quite naturally about things that mean something to them (Holdaway, 1979; Taylor, 1983). The LCT provides a home-like environment in which children choose to write often and naturally.

During the program described here, children wrote in pairs and small groups more often than alone. Some specific writing projects lasted for an entire LCT, and some even extended into later such periods. Projects often culminated in performances presented by their creators to an entire class through such vehicles as puppet shows, roll movies, narrations with musical background, and plays with scenery. The projects were almost always self-sponsored and self-directed by children, as the following incident illustrates.

> Paul said to Kevin, "I'm writin a bunch of stories. Each book is a different part but about the same horse. I have *The Horse Named Jack, Jack Becomes a Police Horse,* and now I'm on the third called *Jack Enters a Horse Race.*"
>
> "Can I read the one where he's a police horse?" Kevin asked.
>
> "OK," Paul answered, "but you really gotta read *The Horse Named Jack* first 'cause they go in order."

As with reading, writing occurred all over the classroom. The table in a typical literacy center's "Author's Spot" could accommodate only about three children at most, so students took to writing while sitting on the floor and at their own desks. Often, they moved desks together to make large working surfaces on which several of them could write at once.

In interviews, teachers and children again said that writing improved because they did so much of it. Teachers also expressed surprise that children who would never write in the traditional classroom setting chose to do so during an LCT. Teachers were amazed, too, at the variety of topics children chose to write about, professing a belief, for instance, that children would never have written about such serious current events topics if they had been assigned by the teacher in the traditional classroom.

While only 24 percent of the recorded incidents involved writing, each incident was so long—often lasting the full 30 minutes of an LCT—that the total time involved came to 3,710 minutes, or about 61 hours. (Morrow, Sharkey, & Firestone, 1993).

Teacher Participation in LCT

In a traditional classroom, rules of classroom interaction established at the beginning of a school year typically constrain the teacher's productivity and creativity as much as the students' (Bossert, 1979). During conventional recitation, for instance, teachers control how long a child may talk as well as the subject matter of verbalization; student opportunities to speak are limited (Sirotnik, 1983). However, limitations also cut into a teacher's effectiveness. Giving too much attention to any one student, for instance, reduces instructional time for others and sometimes even results in a group's loss of focus.

During an LCT, by contrast, a teacher can respond to the needs of one student or a small group without inhibiting the activities or sacrificing the attentiveness-to-task of other students. In fact, the multitask structure of the LCT, with its emphasis on collaborative learning, changes the teacher's role from "sole source" to "guide on the side," that is, the teacher becomes a participant and facilitator. Teachers can more easily recognize and respond to students' emerging insights (Golub, 1988), and can support rather than totally direct efforts at socialization and development of literacy among students. By way of illustration, take the following examples:

> As Mrs. Olsen circulated near where Sarah and Kim were writing a story, Kim asked her how to spell *suddenly*.
>
> Mrs. Olsen spelled the word, then added out of curiosity, "OK, suddenly what?"
>
> Sarah read a portion of their story, and Mrs. Olsen asked, "Since you talk about your sister making you mad in your story, why not write about why she makes you mad?"
>
> "OK," Sarah said. "Let's see, one thing is she just sits by the phone all day long waiting for it to ring for her, and when it does, it is always her friends."
>
> Mrs. Olsen smiled and said, "That would make me angry, too."

Teachers learned to relax during LCT because they could participate, facilitate, and instruct as needed. Perceived by students as friendly and pleasant, they could also be more flexible than during conventional recitation periods. When not working directly with children during LCT teachers often sat among students, reading their own books or writing.

Additional Outcomes

The outcomes that resulted from the contexts and processes generated by the LCT included positive attitudes demonstrated by children in their appreciation of reading and writing, improved reading skills as measured by comprehension tests given in the experimental portion of the research (Morrow, 1992), active participation of children in comprehension activities, the positive literacy behaviors of children who had been identified as having special needs or difficulties in learning, and changes in teacher behavior and in their perceptions of alternative strategies for literacy development.

Appreciation for Reading and Writing

As stated at the outset of this report, a central goal for reading instruction is to develop a reader who has a positive attitude toward reading, appreciates and enjoys reading, and, therefore, will read (Alverman & Guthrie, 1993). Children who associate reading with pleasure will read more and improve their reading ability. The fact that the children who participated in the program described here engaged in literacy activities independently is itself evidence of their positive attitudes toward literacy. Few discipline problems arose during LCT and few children deviated from task. The interview data consistently reflect positive attitudes toward independent reading and writing and reveal reasons for those attitudes.

Sixty-eight of the 98 children interviewed said something similar in essence to "Reading and writing is fun during this time. It makes you happy." Sixty reported something similar in essence to "It makes you like to read and write because you can choose what you want to do and where you want to do it. You can decide to read or write alone or with others. If you work with others, you can decide who with." Teachers generally agreed with the positive statements of the children: that their students liked choices in activity, in work space, and with whom to work, if anyone. The positive appreciation of literature professed in the overwhelming majority of interviews is epitomized in this reported observation:

> Yassin was leaning on a pillow on the carpet reading a story.
>
> He finished reading, sat up, raised the book over his head, and exclaimed out loud but to himself, "This is such a lovely story. It makes me feel so good, I think I'll read it again."
>
> He settled into his former position and began to read.

In all recorded observations, only one percent of the children observed were recorded off-task. All other recorded incidents demonstrated positive attitudes toward reading and writing.

Improved Reading Comprehension, Language, and Writing

Experimental data (Morrow, 1992) demonstrated increased writing ability with significant improvement of the experimental group over the control in the use of story structure elements in written pieces, and in increased vocabulary and language complexity. Children in the treatment groups also demonstrated significant improvement on probed comprehension tests and in story retelling. The qualitative data revealed additional information about comprehension development.

Comprehension occurs at literal, interpretive, and critical levels of understanding. Typically, it is taught by posing questions for children to answer after they have read a passage. Actually, that practice is more of a testing than a teaching approach. There is no assurance that it involves the child in actively constructing meaning from text. By contrast, independent reading and writing activity demonstrates comprehension gains at all three levels, gains apparently achieved spontaneously as students engage in self-selected activities and levels of involvement.

Literal comprehension requires the ability to understand, remember, and demonstrate facts, sequence, and structural elements in a story. That ability is evident in the following episode.

> Christopher and Albert decided to retell a story, *Amelia Bedelia's Family Album* (Parrish, 1988), through a roll movie. Chris told the story as Albert rolled the paper in the roll-movie box to each appropriate scene. Chris demonstrated literal comprehension of the story as he retold it, using dialogue from the book and including other necessary details as he went along.

Inferential comprehension requires children to think beyond text. It calls on such abilities as understanding characters' feelings, predicting outcomes, and putting oneself in the place of a character to determine alternative courses of action. Inferential comprehension requires understanding not explicitly stated or documented in text. The following episode illustrates such understanding.

> Darren read *Frog and Toad Are Friends* (Lobel, 1970). He decided to read it again using puppets. Darren retold the story with the puppets and took the parts of the characters in the story by changing his voice and inferring how they might have sounded. Several children gathered around to watch and listen.

Critical comprehension requires hypothesizing, analyzing, judging, and drawing conclusions. This level of comprehension entails making comparisons and distinguishing fact from opinion. The following incident offers evidence of critical thinking.

> Charlene and Tesha finished reading *Stone Soup* (Linquist, 1970).
>
> Charlene turned back to the part where the soldiers first came into town looking for food, and said, "Tesha, can you believe what those soldiers said, 'We can make soup from a stone'? Those people in that town must be so dumb to believe that. Boy, did those guys fool them! This could never have happened. No one would listen."

Of the 714 recorded incidents in which literacy activities took place, 522 or 74 percent were coded as having documented literal comprehension, 150 or 21 percent interpretive comprehension, and 28 or 4 percent critical comprehension.

For the most part, we think of comprehension development as taking place primarily when teachers ask questions of children. In self-directed activities during LCT in the program described here, however, children demonstrated comprehension of story in almost every incident recorded. None involved the necessary presence of a teacher, nor a lesson prepared in advance by a teacher armed with questions and prescribed responses. Our interview data reveal that children were aware that their comprehension was enhanced during independent reading and writing. When asked, "What do you learn during LCT?" 40 of 98 children responded that you learn to understand what you are reading and you learn a lot of new words. All teachers said that children enhanced their comprehension, sense of story structure, and vocabulary development during LCT.

Gains among Children with Special Needs

Data gathered from this program by direct observation and videotape also revealed that children increased their voluntary participation in cooperative literacy activity in spite of the fact that many of them had previously been identified as children with special needs. A large percentage attended basic-skills (Chapter 1) classes because their development in reading and writing had been considered below grade level, or they were enrolled in English as a Second Language (ESL) classes, or they had been classified as having social and emotional problems. Some fell into more than one of these categories.

Yet, they participated in LCT with peers who had not been assigned to any of those special categories. In fact, third-party observers usually could not tell which students fell into such classifications until classroom teachers pointed them out. Often, children who had been assigned those special classifications emerged as leaders; they found activities in which they excelled, their special needs often not at all obvious. The following anecdotes illustrate the literacy behaviors demonstrated by children with special needs.

> Patrick was repeating second grade and receiving basic skills instruction. He emerged as a leader during LCT, frequently organizing and carrying out projects with groups of children. When he decided that he wanted to make a roll movie, he was able to entice Tarene, Neela, Elvira, and Corine to work with him. He picked the story *Bedtime for Frances* (Hoban, 1960). He delegated responsibility to those involved, determining, for example, who should draw which picture and why the color yellow should not be used because it wouldn't show up very well. The project took a week to complete. It was presented to the class with each child reading the portion of the book that went with the illustration he or she had done.

> Tina entered the class midyear, at first a nonparticipant who spoke only Spanish. During LCT, Tina would choose a book from the literacy center and look at the pictures. One day she inched slowly over to two girls who were doing a puppet show. Esther asked Tina if she wanted to have a puppet to help. Tina smiled, so Esther gave her a puppet and showed her how to use it on the puppet stage. Although she did not use any dialogue, she moved the puppet around when it was her turn to participate, and Esther did the talking.

Jack had been classified as autistic. In routine instruction he never spoke nor did he interact with other children. During LCT, on the other hand, he always went to the "Author's Spot" and wrote stories that he hung on the bulletin board in a space left for children to post their work. From time to time, other children sat next to him, and he was observed on several occasions reading his stories to children who had asked him to do so. He was also observed talking about his work with other children. But Jack neither spoke nor interacted with anyone else at any other time during the entire school day.

Thirty children in the study had been identified as having special needs. During the study, every one of them was observed participating in literacy behavior of one form or another. During interviews, teachers commented that there seemed to be something for everyone during LCT. Children lacking in basic skills and considered "at risk" found literacy activities which they could enjoy and at which they could succeed. ESL children found ways to participate, and the environment appeared excellent for enhancing language development. Children with emotional problems, who normally tended to be withdrawn or to reveal disruptive personalities, became productive participants.

While children with special needs participated in literacy activities, they often did so through manipulatives, apparently a motivating factor for them.

Change in Teacher Behavior and Beliefs about Literacy Development

Teachers acted as facilitators, instructors, and participants during LCT. They helped children get organized, they gave instructional assistance when it was asked for, they participated in activities with children, and they read on their own. Participants in a social setting, they interacted in a friendly manner with students.

As reported earlier in this monograph, comments of the six teachers who participated in the program were extremely consistent during their interviews. In general, teachers reported initial skepticism about the amount of time the program would take away from other classroom activities (e.g., basal reading instruction), but they added that by the end of the experiment, they saw literature as an integral part of reading instruction. All reported prior concerns about getting children to work on tasks independently during the LCT, but all six were able to work such problems through with time. All planned to continue the program and to further integrate literature with their basal instruction. When asked what they learned from participating in the program, it was apparent that they had changed some of their beliefs about literacy instruction, for they described specific changes in their own behavior and attitudes. Among their responses:

> Children are capable of cooperating and collaborating independently in reading and writing activities and of learning from each other.
>
> In an atmosphere that provides choices in activity and with whom one works, children of all ability levels chose to work together, a situation that does not normally occur.
>
> There is something for everyone in the program, advanced and slower children alike.
>
> It is the first time that I realized how important it is for me to model reading and writing for children and to interact with them during LCT.
>
> It made me more flexible and spontaneous and a facilitator of learning rather than always teaching.
>
> I learned that the basal serves to organize children's skill development, specifically in the area of word recognition. The literature program emphasizes vocabulary and comprehension. The programs complement each other and should be used simultaneously.
>
> Children who don't readily participate in reading and writing did so during the LCT. I think that is because they were the ones making the decisions about what they would do.

6 Discussion: Implications of the Results of the Study

Literacy Performance

The implementation of regularly scheduled literature-based activities and the creation of appealing, carefully designed literacy centers with opportunities to engage in periods of social collaborative reading and writing led to a substantial increase in children's literacy performance on several measures. On all three comprehension measures, the probed recall, and the oral and written retellings, children in the two experimental groups scored better than those in the control group, although there were no differences in performance between the two experimental groups. Mean scores for children in the school-based-only program were higher than scores for those in the home-and-school program, but not with significant difference. In the category of resolution in oral and written retellings, however, the home-and-school group did score significantly better than the control and the school-based-only groups.

Similar results were obtained on oral and written creation of original stories. Both experimental groups scored significantly better than the control, but did not differ from each other. A close look at the means for the two experimental groups, however, showed that youngsters in the home-and-school program scored higher than youngsters in the school-based-only program.

Analysis of language complexity and vocabulary development indicated that experimental groups used a greater variety of words in written story retellings, and in both written and oral original stories than the control group. On the other hand, there were no significant differences among the groups in the variety of words used in oral story retellings. T-unit analysis indicated that experimental groups used significantly longer T-units than did the control group in oral and written original stories, and in written retelling, but, again, there were no significant differences among groups in oral story retelling. It is interesting to note that scores on tests that involved writing increased more than scores on oral tests, a phenomenon also evident in the measures of language complexity.

The study did not demonstrate that the home-and-school program was superior to the school-only program. Means for the home-and-school program were slightly higher than those for school-only, but not significantly different. Of the 56 families assigned to the parent component, 38 were represented in the workshops provided. In spite of follow-up phone calls and materials mailed and sent home with children, it appears that home involvement was not sufficient to demonstrate any effect. Home involvement is, however, an important issue. I am convinced that parental participation would make a difference. We need to find ways to get parents involved to enhance literacy in general.

No differences were found between the experimental and control groups on the standardized tests, a result that is not surprising since standardized measures have not been sensitive to literature instruction. However, it can be observed that children in the experimental groups performed as well on standardized tests as did children in the control group, and better on other measures of literacy used in the study. One might have expected that the control group would have scored better on the standardized test, since their instruction reflected the nature of that test. The results in this study and in other similar work (Morrow, O'Connor, & Smith, 1990; Walmsley & Walp, 1990) indicate that literature-based instruction does not diminish reading achievement test scores, and there seems to be an advantage in combining a literature program with basal instruction.

Literacy Performance of Children from Diverse Backgrounds

The literature review at the beginning of this paper addressed issues that have been raised by other authors concerning the effect of a literature-based, process-oriented program on children from diverse backgrounds. One concern was whether minority students could demonstrate improvement in literacy achievement in this type of setting, with instructional materials, specifically children's literature, that might not be familiar to them and instruction and social settings that might not provide direct skill strategies.

A comparison of scores from nine tests that examined literacy development revealed that the black and white children performed similarly in the experimental and control groups in pre- and post-tests. The standard deviations and range of scores were also similar between the different cultural groups. It appears that concerns about literature-based instruction involving a social collaborative component and the achievement of children from diverse backgrounds are unfounded for the type of program studied in this investigation. In reflecting on the components of the program, I have tried to establish reasons for its success. The observational data revealed that the children worked in groups and that the teachers worked with them by demonstrating, facilitating, and participating in literature activities, thereby exhibiting high expectations for student performance. They offered support and constructive feedback when needed during Literacy Center Time (LCT). The groups were always representative of the diversity in the classroom-at-large. One might conclude that the blending of many backgrounds helped students help each other with the focus on traditional American story structure required in some of the tests. Further, the program did feature selected pieces of literature from cultural backgrounds represented by students themselves. This inclusion may have made the children more comfortable with the use of children's literature in general and more receptive to its varied forms and characteristics.

The basal reader was also used in all experimental groups, although not as much time was spent with it in the treatment rooms as in the control group. It seems that there might have been enough direct instruction of skill strategies when using the basal to complement the literature-based program and enable the children in minority groups to succeed. It may also be that a balance of effective and varied instructional strategies within a literacy program will work well for children regardless of their background.

A second concern about this type of program is the ability of minority children to function in a process environment where choices and responsibility for self-direction are provided, rather than explicit instructions for proceeding with a task. The observational data revealed that children in the study, regardless of their backgrounds, were able to function in this setting. During LCT, children had to make choices and direct their own activities. To enable youngsters to function effectively, rules were established concerning what children could and should do, as described in Chapter 2. Although the program allowed choices, explicit rules helped to direct behavior. Montessori theory (1965) was incorporated through the creation of environments that took into consideration the necessity for active learning and an organizational system that allowed freedom within limits through rules such as (a) take only one material at a time, (b) replace materials to their exact spot before taking another, (c) remain on task, and (d) work quietly. Montessori designed her strategies for children from disadvantaged backgrounds whose home environments lacked direction and structure, similar to the home environments of some children in the study.

Since neither the children nor the teachers who participated in this investigation were at first familiar with the organizational strategy on which the literature-based program depended, rules were reviewed prior to each period, and teachers helped children with their choices and selections when necessary. There were some problems with on-task behavior early in the program, but within a month—once rules had been firmly established, literacy behaviors modeled by teachers, and teachers had been seen as facilitators and participators—children were able to function within the setting. Elements of Teale's, Holdaway's, and Cambourne's theories for literacy learning were embedded in the program as children observed literate behaviors, collaborated, practiced skills, and took responsibility for their learning. It appears to me, from the formal observations of the youngsters, that appropriate behavior in this setting was dependent on good classroom management organized by the teacher rather than on a child's cultural background.

Children's Use of Literature

The survey of after-school activities, ability to name book titles, authors, and illustrators, and reported use of books read at home and in school demonstrated that the use of books increased among children in the experimental groups over the period of the study. One of the most interesting results from these data was that children reported not only an increased reading of books at home, but a significant increase in magazine reading as well, even though magazine reading was found to have very low priority in the pretest. A home subscription to a children's magazine had been provided during the study for all children in the experimental groups, a move that apparently had an impact on their reading habits. Children were observed bringing their magazines to school to show what they had received at home. Many of them had never before received mail and very proudly pointed out their names on the mailing labels.

Attitudes Toward Reading and the Literature Program

The interview data pertaining to attitudes toward reading instruction and the literature program were rich with information, with consistency between responses of teachers and children. Strong trends emerged as well. All components of the literature program (such components as literacy centers, teachers reading to children, and independent reading and writing periods) strongly impressed both children and teachers. Most of the children identified reading and writing in the literature program as fun. Answers to other questions revealed what they apparently meant by "fun." Reading and writing were "fun" when you could choose what you wanted to read and write, whether to work alone or with others, and whether or not to use literature manipulatives such as puppets, roll movies, and feltboards. Reading and writing were "fun" because of comfortable surroundings in the literacy center, in the author's spot, on a rug, in a rocking chair, in a quiet corner, or at your desk. Reading and writing were "fun" because in this atmosphere children taught each other, and teachers interacted in positive ways with children, working along with them. Teachers reinforced such observations and recognized that reading skills were still being developed. Children, too, articulated what they felt they were learning.

Interview data also indicated that teachers shared some concerns about the program, such as finding time for literature-based activities and independent reading and writing periods, accommodating both literature and basal instruction, and helping children work independently on-task and productively.

Observational Data

The presentation of the observational data in the results section provides an in-depth look at the richness of the interaction that occurred during LCT and how this portion of the intervention provided the practice in literacy activity that contributed to increased literacy performance. These qualitative data provide additional important information concerning the use of the environment, social interactions between children, and teacher behavior in directed literature activities and during LCT.

The literature-based reading program reported here was not intended to take the place of more traditional literacy instruction. Nevertheless, when children were given the chance to select their activities and work with others, a great deal of self-sponsored social literacy behavior occurred. Our findings suggest that (1) the physical design of the literacy centers and the materials within them, plus (2) teacher modeling of pleasurable storybook reading and the use of literature manipulatives, and (3) time for children to work within such an environment, motivated socially interactive literacy activity which in turn led to the increased literacy performance documented (Morrow, 1992). Beyond those documented cognitive gains, positive attitudes toward reading and writing were apparent in the enthusiasm of children as they participated in LCT and in their comments during interviews. Further, the freedom to select that was inherent in LCT was at least as important to the children as was the manipulative nature of many of the available materials and the activities suggested.

Components of the reading process most difficult to document in our analyses of the program's results concerned word recognition and the acquisition of knowledge about print. However, one can infer from the amount of oral and silent reading that took place, from recorded evidence of comprehension, and from the nature of writing activities, that children were developing word recognition skills within the program. Context clues and sound-symbol relationships, for instance, are a priori necessities to the extensive reading, comprehension, and writing documented during the literature-based social collaborative LCT activities.

That the program was particularly effective for children with learning difficulties, allowing them to engage enjoyably in literacy activities with peers whose abilities differed from their own and to do so with no disruption, might be attributed to the absence of stigma, the common use of reward, and the intrinsic nature of much of that reward as they completed tasks successfully. Moreover, the choice offered by the program facilitated the capabilities of children with learning problems. The choices given them during LCT were substantial in comparison to the essential lack of choice inherent in traditional reading instruction, based as it is on teacher-assigned work, but the choices were also offered within clear limits. The program's combination of consistent rules, teacher roles in modeling and facilitating, and active involvement of children helped students manage the decisions they had to make. Again, it seems likely that good classroom management by the teachers helped overcome the control problems normally attributed to a child's learning problems or cultural background.

What occurred during LCT reflects Holdaway's (1979) theory of developmental learning as characterized by (1) self-regulated, individualized activities and (2) frequent social interaction with peers and adults in (3) an environment rich with materials, an environment in which holistic acts of reading and writing can occur by choice. He defines four processes that enable children to acquire literacy abilities, all of which were provided during independent reading and writing periods: (1) observation of literacy behaviors, (2) collaboration in literacy activities through social interaction with peers or adults, (3) practice as children try out what they have learned, and (4) performance which allows a child to share what has been learned and to obtain approval from supportive, interested peers and adults.

The social collaborative LCT component also demonstrated the principles of good job design. Hackman and Oldham (1980) maintain that people are intrinsically motivated to succeed at high levels when three conditions are met. First, the work must be meaningful and significant to the worker, allowing use of a variety of skills to accomplish whole identifiable results. Second, the worker must be given a measure of autonomy in order to feel responsibility for the work. Finally, the worker must receive feedback and a sense of accomplishment, preferably intrinsically, from the task itself, but also from peers and supervisors. Many educators are reluctant to allow children to make decisions about their own learning. Many of us are reluctant to let them participate in self-directed cooperative situations that we fear will reduce teachers' sense of control and make the school look disorganized. The results of this study challenge those fears. They indicate, rather, that with time and appropriate environmental preparation, children can and will engage in productive, self-directed literacy activities, both alone and collaboratively, and that such participation can increase their interest in and capacity for reading and writing.

A limitation of this investigation that should be addressed in future research is the effect of such a program with the use of more expository materials. Although such material was available to children, it was not featured as often as narrative texts. In addition there were no measures incorporated to deal specifically with the effect of expository material. There is a great deal to be gained from both narrative and expository material, and both should be given appropriate consideration in literacy instruction. Because the author developed the study as a literature-enriched program embedded in a reading program, the integration of informational expository material was not given as much emphasis as narratives.

Overall results suggest that the combination of the literature-based instruction used with its varied components balanced with traditional basal reading instruction is more powerful than traditional instruction alone. This investigation strengthens the claim for the inclusion of literature and social collaboration as an integral part of reading instruction with children from varied backgrounds. The study provides an illustration of a balanced approach to literacy instruction with the use of both literature and more traditional basal reading materials. There has been a great deal of discussion recently concerning more balanced approaches for literacy development with the widespread use of whole language practices that placed little emphasis on explicit skill instruction. The positive results of this study with the diverse population involved suggests that more research needs to be done to determine if the more balanced approach used in this investigation is preferable to classrooms that have completely embraced holistic instructional strategies.

Appendix
Storybooks Used for Testing

Probed Comprehension Test

Pretest:

Fujikawa, G. (1980). *Jenny learns a lesson.* New York: Grossett & Dunlap.

Post-test:

Hurd, R. (1980). *Under the lemon tree.* Boston: Little Brown.

Oral Retelling Test

Pretest:

Flory, J. (1980). *The bear on the doorstep.* Boston: Houghton Mifflin.

Post-test:

Keller, H. (1980). *Cromwell's glasses.* New York: Greenwillow Books.

Written Retelling Test

Pretest:

Bourgeois, P. (1986). *Franklin in the dark.* New York: Scholastic.

Post-test:

Zolotow, C. (1962). *Mr. Rabbit and the lovely present.* New York: Harper & Row.

References

Alverman, D. E., & Guthrie, J. T. (1993). *Themes and directions of the National Reading Research Center* (Perspectives No. 1). Athens, GA: National Reading Research Center, Universities of Georgia and Maryland.

Alverman, D. E., O'Brien, D. G., & Dillon, D. R. (1990). What teachers do when they say they're having discussions of content area reading assignments: A qualitative analysis. *Reading Research Quarterly, 25,* 296–322.

Anderson, R. C., Wilson, P. T., & Fielding, L. G. (1988). Growth in reading and how children spend their time outside of school. *Reading Research Quarterly, 23,* 285–303.

Augustine, D., Gruber, K., & Hanson, L. (1989, December). Cooperation works! *Educational Leadership, 46,* 4–7.

Barker, L. L. (1963). *The stream of behavior: Explorations of its structure and content.* New York: Appleton-Century-Crofts.

Bergeron, B. S. (1990). What does the term whole language mean? Constructing a definition from the literature. *Journal of Reading Behavior, 22,* 301–329.

Bissett, D. (1969). The amount and effect of recreational reading in selected fifth grade classes. Unpublished doctoral dissertation, Syracuse University, New York.

Bogdan, R., & Biklen, S. K. (1982). *Qualitative research for education: An introduction to theory and methods.* Boston: Allyn & Bacon.

Book Industry Study Group. (1984). *The 1983 consumer research study on reading and book publishing.* New York: Book Industry Study Group.

Bossert, S. T. (1979). *Tasks and social relationships in classrooms.* Cambridge: Cambridge University Press.

Brandt, D. (1990). *Literacy as involvement: The acts of writers, readers, and texts.* Carbondale, IL: Southern Illinois University Press.

Cambourne, B. (1988). *The whole story: Natural learning and the acquisition of literacy in the classroom.* New York: Ashton Scholastic.

Cazden, C. B. (1986). Classroom discourse. In M. C. Wittrock (Ed.), *The handbook of research in teaching* (3rd ed., pp. 432–463). New York: Macmillan.

Childers, P. R., & Ross, J. (1973). The relationship between viewing television and school achievement. *The Journal of Educational Research, 66,* 317–319.

Chomsky, C. (1972). Stages in language development and reading exposure. *Harvard Educational Review, 42,* 1–33.

Clark, M. M. (1976). *Young fluent readers.* London: Heinemann Educational Books.

Clay, M. (1976). Early childhood and cultural diversity in New Zealand. *Reading Teacher, 29,* 333–342.

Corsaro, W. (1985). *Friendship and peer culture in the early years.* Norwood, NJ: Ablex.

Cullinan, B. (Ed.). (1987). *Children's literature in the reading program.* Newark, DE: International Reading Association.

Delpit, L. D. (1986). Skills and other dilemmas of a progressive black educator. *Harvard Educational Review, 56,* 379–385.

Delpit, L. D. (1988). The silenced dialogue: Power and pedagogy in educating other people's children. *Harvard Educational Review, 58,* 280–297.

Delpit, L. D. (1991). A conversation with Lisa Delpit. *Language Arts, 68,* 541–547.

Dewey, J. (1916). *Democracy and education.* New York: Macmillan.

Dodge, M., & Frost, J. (1986). Children's dramatic play: Influence of thematic and non-thematic settings. *Childhood Education, 62,* 166–170.

Durkin, D. (1974–1975). A six year study of children who learned to read in school at the age of four. *Reading Research Quarterly, 10,* 9–61.

Felsenthal, H. (1989). The tradebook as an instructional tool: Strategies in approaching literature. In J. W. Stewig & S. L. Sebesta (Eds.), *Using literature in the elementary classroom* (pp. 35–54). Urbana, IL: National Council of Teachers of English.

Fetterman, D. M. (1984). *Ethnography in educational evaluation.* Beverly Hills, CA: Sage Publications.

Field, T. (1980). Preschool play: Effects of teacher/child ratios and organization of classroom space. *Child Study Journal, 10,* 191–205.

Ford, M. E. (1992). *Motivating humans: Goals, emotions, and personal agency beliefs.* Newbury Park, CA: Sage Publications.

Forman, E., & Cazden, C. (1985). Exploring Vygotskian perspectives in education: The cognitive value of peer interaction. In J. Wertsch (Ed.), *Culture, communication, and cognition. Vygotskian perspectives* (323–347). Cambridge: Cambridge University Press.

Froebel, F. (1974). *The education of man.* Clifton, NJ: Augustus M. Kelly.

Gambrell, L. B., Almasi, J. F., Xie, Q., & Heland, V. (in press). Helping first-graders get off to a running start in reading: A home-school-community program that enhances family literacy. In L. M. Morrow (Ed.), *Family liter-*

acy: Multiple perspectives to enhance literacy development. Newark, DE: International Reading Association.

Gambrell, L. B., Kapinus, B. A., & Koskinen, P. S. (1991). Retelling and the reading comprehension of proficient and less proficient readers. *Journal of Educational Research, 84,* 356–362.

Gambrell, L. B., Palmer, B. M., & Coding, R. M. (1993). *Motivation to read.* Washington, DC: Office of Educational Research and Improvement.

Golub, J. (Ed.). (1988). *Focus on collaborative learning.* Urbana, IL: National Council of Teachers of English.

Goodman, K. S. (1989a). Whole-language research: Foundations of development. *Elementary School Journal, 90,* 207–220.

Goodman, Y. M. (1989b). Roots of the whole language movement. *The Elementary School Journal, 90,* 113–127.

Graves, D. H. (1975). An examination of the writing process of seven-year-old children. *Research in the Teaching of English, 9,* 227–241.

Greaney, V. (1980). Factors related to amount and type of leisure reading. *Reading Research Quarterly, 15,* 337–357.

Greaney, V., & Hegarty, M. (1987). Correlates of leisure-time reading. *Journal of Research in Reading, 10,* 3–20.

Green, J. L., & Wallat, C. (Eds.). (1981). *Ethnography and language in educational settings.* Norwood, NJ: Ablex.

Hackman, J. R., & Oldham, G. R. (1980). *Work: Redesigned.* Reading, MA: Addison Wesley.

Hoffman, J. V., Roser, N. L., & Farest, C. (1988). Literature sharing strategies in classrooms serving students from economically disadvantaged and language different home environments. In J. E. Readance & R. S. Baldwin (Eds.), *Dialogues in literacy research. Thirty-seventh yearbook of the National Reading Conference* (pp. 331–338). Chicago: National Reading Conference.

Holdaway, D. (1979). *The foundations of literacy.* New York: Ashton Scholastic.

Huck, C. (1976). *Children's literature in the elementary school* (3rd ed.). New York: Holt, Rinehart & Winston.

Hunt, K. (1965). Grammatical structures written at three grade levels (Research Report No. 3). Champaign, IL: National Council of Teachers of English.

Irving, A. (1980). *Promoting voluntary reading for children and young people.* Paris: Unesco.

Jett-Simpson, M. (1989). Creative drama and story comprehension. In J. W. Stewig & S. L. Sebesta (Eds.), *Using literature in the elementary classroom* (pp. 91–109). Urbana, IL: National Council of Teachers of English.

Johnson, D. W., & Johnson, R. T. (1981). Effects of cooperative and individualistic learning experiences on interethnic interaction. *Journal of Educational Psychology, 73,* 444–449.

Johnson, D. W., & Johnson, R. T. (1987). *Learning together and alone: Cooperative, competitive, and individualistic learning.* (2nd ed.). Englewood Cliffs, NJ: Prentice Hall.

Johnson, D. W., Maruyama, G., Johnson, R., Nelson, D., & Skon, L. (1981). Effects of cooperative, competitive, and individualistic goal structures on achievement: A meta-analysis. *Psychological Bulletin, 89,* 47–62.

Kagan, S., Zahn, G. L., Widaman, K. F., Schwarzwald, J., & Tyrrell, G. (1985). Classroom structural bias: Impact of cooperative and competitive classroom structures on cooperative and competitive individuals and groups. In R. Slavin, S. Sharan, S. Kagan, R. Hertz Lazarowitz, C. Webb, & R. Schmuck (Eds.), *Learning to cooperate, cooperating to learn* (pp. 277–312). New York: Plenum.

La Freniere, P., Strayer, F. F., & Gauthier, R. (1984). The emergence of same-sex affiliative preferences among preschool peers: A developmental/ethological perspective. *Child Development, 55,* 1958–1965.

Lamme, L. (1976). Are reading habits and abilities related? *Reading Teacher, 30,* 21–27.

Lew, M., Mesch, D., Johnson, D. W., & Johnson, R. (1986). Positive interdependence, academic and collaborative-skills group contingencies, and isolated students. *American Educational Research Journal, 23,* 476–488.

Library of Congress. (1984). Books in our future: A report to the Congress from the Librarian of Congress. Washington, DC: Joint Committee on the Library, Congress of the U.S.

Lincoln, Y. S., & Guba, E. G. (1985). *Naturalistic inquiry.* Beverly Hills, CA: Sage Publications.

Long, H., & Henderson, E. H. (1973). Children's uses of time: Some personal and social correlates. *Elementary School Journal, 73,* 193–199.

Loughlin, C. E., & Martin, M. D. (1987). *Supporting literacy: Developing effective learning environments.* New York: Teachers College Press.

Maehr, M. L. (1976). Continuing motivation: An analysis of a seldom considered educational outcome. *Review of Educational Research, 46,* 443–462.

Mandler, J., & Johnson, N. (1977). Remembrance of things parsed: Story structure and recall. *Cognitive Psychology, 9,* 111–151.

Manley, M. A., & Simon, E. A. (1980). A reading celebration from K to 8. *Reading Teacher, 33,* 552–554.

McCombs, B. L. (1989). Self-regulated learning and academic achievement: A phenomenological view. In B. J. Zimmerman & D. H. Schunk (Eds.), *Self-regulated learning and academic achievement: Theory, research, and practice* (pp. 51–82). New York: Springer-Verlag.

Michaels, S. (1984). Listening and responding: Hearing the logic in children's classroom narrative. *Theory into Practice, 23,* 218–223.

Miles, M. B., & Huberman, A. M. (1984). Drawing valid meaning from qualitative data: Towards a shared craft. *Educational Researcher, 13,* 20–30.

Monson, D., & Sebesta, S. (1991). Reading preferences. In J. Flood, J. Jensen, D. Lapp, & J. Squire (Eds.), *Handbook of research on teaching the English language arts* (pp. 664–673). New York: Macmillan.

Montessori, M. (1965). *Spontaneous activity in education.* New York: Schocken Books.

Moore, G. (1986). Effects of the spatial definition of behavior settings on children's behavior: A quasi-experimental field study. *Journal of Environmental Psychology, 6,* 205–231.

Morrow, L. M. (1983). Home and school correlates of early interest in literature. *Journal of Educational Research, 76,* 221–230.

Morrow, L. M. (1984). Reading stories to young children: Effects of story structure and traditional questioning strategies on comprehension. *Journal of Reading Behavior, 16,* 273–288.

Morrow, L. M. (1985). Retelling stories: A strategy for improving young children's comprehension, concept of story structure, and oral language complexity. *The Elementary School Journal, 85,* 661–674.

Morrow, L. M. (1986). Voluntary reading: Forgotten goal. *Educational Forum, 50,* 159–168.

Morrow, L. M. (1990). The impact of classroom environmental changes on the promotion of literacy during play. *Early Childhood Research Quarterly, 5,* 537–554.

Morrow, L. M. (1992). The impact of a literature-based program on literacy achievement, use of literature, and attitudes of children from minority backgrounds. *Reading Research Quarterly, 27,* 250–275.

Morrow, L. M. (1992). *Literacy development in the early years: Helping children read and write* (3rd ed.). Boston: Allyn & Bacon.

Morrow, L. M., O'Connor, E. M., & Smith, J. (1990). Effects of a storyreading program on the literacy development of at-risk kindergarten children. *Journal of Reading Behavior, 20,* 104–141.

Morrow, L. M., Sharkey, E., & Firestone, W. A. (1993). *Promoting independent reading and writing through self-directed literacy activities in a collaborative setting.* Reading Research Report #2. University of Georgia and Maryland: National Reading Research Center.

Morrow, L. M., & Smith, J. K. (1988). The effects of group setting on interactive storybook reading. *Reading Research Quarterly, 25,* 213–231.

Morrow, L. M., & Weinstein, C. S. (1986). Encouraging voluntary reading: The impact of a literature program on children's use of library centers. *Reading Research Quarterly, 21,* 330–346.

National Academy of Education. Commission on Reading. (1985). *Becoming a nation of readers: The report of the Commission on Reading*. Washington, DC: ERIC.

Neuman, S. B. (1980). Television: Its effects on reading and school achievement. *The Reading Teacher, 34,* 801–805.

Neuman, S., & Roskos, K. (1990). The influence of literacy-enriched play settings on preschoolers' engagement with written language. In J. Zutell & S. McCormick (Eds.), *Literacy theory and research: Analyses from multiple paradigms* (pp. 179–187). 39th Yearbook of the National Reading Conference, Chicago.

Neuman, S., & Roskos, K. (1992). Literacy objects as cultural tools: Effects on children's literacy behaviors in play. *Reading Research Quarterly, 27,* 203–225.

O'Donnell, R., Griffin, J., & Norris, C. (1967). *Syntax of kindergarten and elementary school children: A transformational analysis* (Research Report No. 3). Champaign, IL: National Council of Teachers of English.

O'Flahavan, J., Gambrell, L. B., Guthrie, J., Stahl, S., & Alverman, D. (1992, April). Poll results guide activities of research center. *Reading Today* (p. 12). Newark, DE: International Reading Association.

Oldfather, P. (1993). What students say about motivating experiences in a whole language classroom. *The Reading Teacher, 46,* 672–681.

Patton, M. Q. (1990). *Qualitative evaluation and research methods* (2nd ed.). Newbury Park, CA: Sage Publications.

Pelligrini, A. (1980). The relationship between kindergarteners' play and achievement in prereading, language, and writing. *Psychology in the Schools, 17,* 530–535.

Pelligrini, A., & Galda, L. (1982). The effects of thematic fantasy play training on the development of children's story comprehension. *American Educational Research Journal, 19,* 443–452.

Phyfe-Perkins, E. (1979). *Application of the behavior-person-environment paradigm to the analysis and evaluation of early childhood education programs*. Unpublished Ed.D. dissertation, University of Massachusetts.

Piaget, J. (1959). *The language and thought of the child* (3rd ed.). London: Routledge & Kegan Paul.

Piaget, J., & Inhelder, B. (1969). *The psychology of the child*. New York: Basic Books.

Rivlin, L., & Weinstein, C. S. (1984). Educational issues, school settings, and environmental psychology. *Journal of Environmental Psychology, 4,* 347–364.

Rodin, J., Rennert, K., & Solomon, S. (1980). Intrinsic motivation for control: Fact or fiction. In A. Baum, J. E. Singer, & S. Valois (Eds.), *Advances in environmental psychology*. Hillsdale, NJ: Erlbaum.

Rosenthal, B. A. (1973). An ecological study of free play in the nursery school. Unpublished doctoral dissertation, Wayne State University, Detroit.

Rossman, G. B., & Wilson, B. L. (1985). Numbers and words: Combining quantitative and qualitative methods in a single large-scale evaluation study. *Evaluation Review, 9,* 627–643.

Rusk, R., & Scotland, J. (1979). *Doctrines of the great educators.* New York: St. Martin's Press.

Saltz, E., & Johnson, J. (1974). Training for the thematic-fantasy play in culturally disadvantaged children. Preliminary results. *Journal of Educational Psychology, 66,* 623–630.

Scallon, R., & Scallon, S. B. K. (1984). Cook it up and boiling it down. Abstracts in Athabaskan children's story retelling. In D. Tanner (Ed.), *Coherence in spoken and written discourse* (pp. 173–195). (*Advances in Discourse Practices, XII*). Norwood, NJ: Ablex.

Sirotnik, K. A. (1983). What you see is what you get: Consistency, persistency, and mediocracy in classrooms. *Harvard Educational Review, 53,* 16-31.

Slavin, R. E. (1983). Non-cognitive outcomes. In J. M. Levine & M. C. Wang (Eds.), *Teacher and student perceptions: Implications for learning* (pp. 341–366). Hillsdale, NJ: Erlbaum Associates.

Slavin, R. E. (1990). *Cooperative learning: Theory, research, and practice.* Englewood Cliffs, NJ: Prentice Hall.

Spaulding, C. I. (1992). The motivation to read and write. In J. W. Irwin & M. A. Doyle (Eds.), *Reading/writing connections: Learning from research* (pp. 177–201). Newark, DE: International Reading Association.

Spiegel, D. L. (1981). *Reading for pleasure: Guidelines.* Newark, DE: International Reading Association.

Spiegel, D., & Whaley, J. (1980, December). *Evaluating comprehension skills by sensitizing students to structural aspects of narratives.* Paper presented at the National Reading Conference, San Diego, CA.

Spielberg, S. (1987). Acceptance speech at the Academy Awards. Los Angeles, CA.

Spivak, M. (1973). Archetypal place. *Architectual Forum, 40,* 40–44.

Taylor, B. M., Frye, B. J., & Maruyama, G. M. (1990). Time spent reading and reading growth. *American Educational Research Journal, 27*(2), 351–362.

Taylor, D. (1983). *Family literacy: Young children learn to read and write.* Exeter, NH: Heinemann.

Teale, W. (1982). Toward a theory of how children learn to read and write naturally. *Language Arts, 59,* 555–570.

Teale, W. (1984). Reading to young children: Its significance for literacy development. In H. Goelman, A. Oberg, & F. Smith (Eds.), *Awakening to literacy* (pp. 110–121). Exeter, NH: Heinemann Educational Books.

Teale, W., & Sulzby, E. (Eds.). (1986). *Emergent literacy: Writing and reading.* Norwood, NJ: Ablex.

Thorndyke, P. (1977). Cognitive structures in comprehension and memory of narrative discourse. *Cognitive Psychology, 9,* 77–110.

Turner, J. C. (1992, April). Identifying motivation for literacy in first grade: An observational study. Paper presented at the annual meeting of the American Educational Research Association, San Francisco.

Vygotsky, L. S. (1978). *Mind and society: The development of higher psychological processes.* Cambridge, MA: Harvard University Press.

Walberg, H. J., & Tsai, S. (1984). Reading achievement and diminishing returns to time. *Journal of Educational Psychology, 76,* 442–451.

Walmsley, S. A., & Walp, T. P. (1990). Integrating literature and composing into the language arts curriculum: Philosophy and practice. *Elementary School Journal, 90,* 251–274.

Whitehead, F., Capey, A. C., & Maddren, W. (1975). *Children's reading interests.* London, UK: Evans and Matheun.

Winer, B. J. (1971). *Statistical principles in experimental design* (2nd ed.). New York: McGraw-Hill.

Wittrock, M. C. (Ed.). (1986). *Handbook of research on teaching* (3rd ed.). New York: Macmillan.

Wood, K. (1990). Collaborative learning. *Reading Teacher,* 346–347.

Woodward, C. (1984). Guidelines for facilitating sociodramatic play. *Childhood Education, 60,* 172–177.

Yager, S., Johnson, D. W., & Johnson, R. T. (1985). Oral discussion, group-to-individual transfer, and achievement in cooperative learning groups. *Journal of Educational Psychology, 77,* 60–66.

Children's Literature References

Aardema, V. (1989). *Bringing the rain to Kapiti Plain.* New York: Scholastic.

Cole, J. (1990). *The magic school bus, lost in the solar system.* New York: Scholastic.

Eastman, P. D. (1960). *Are you my mother?* New York: Random House.

Galdone, P. (1971). *The three bears.* New York: Scholastic.

Galdone, P. (1975). *The gingerbread boy.* New York: Seabury Press.

Hoban, R. (1960). *Bedtime for Frances.* New York: Harper & Row.

Johnson, C. (1955). *Harold and the purple crayon.* New York: Harper & Row.

Keats, E. (1968). *A letter to Amy.* New York: Harper & Row.

Kessler, L. P. (1966). *Kick, pass, and run.* New York: Harper & Row.

Linquist, W. (1970). *Stone soup.* New York: Western Publishing Co.

Lobel, A. (1970). *Frog and toad are friends.* New York: HarperCollins.

Parish, P. (1988). *Amelia Bedelia's family album.* New York: Greenwillow Books.

Piper, W. (1954). *The little engine that could.* New York: Platt & Munk.

Seuss, D. (1960). *Green eggs and ham.* New York: Random House.

Stevens, J. (1971). *The tortoise and the hare.* New York: Holiday Books.

Stobbs, W. (1970). *Rumpelstiltskin.* New York: Walck.

Zolotow, C. (1962). *Mr. Rabbit and the lovely present.* New York: Harper & Row

Index

Collaborative literacy settings, 59 fig. 1
Comfort, in literacy centers, 25, 50, 52, 78
Comprehension
  development with props, 11
  and engaged readers, 1
  enhancement of, 50, 51
  evaluation of, 33–34, 38
  levels of, 69–70
Conflicts, within groups, 63–64
Constructive feedback, 76, 80
Content-area learning, 8
Context clues, 79
Control groups, 32, 36, 44 table 4, 74, 75
Cooperation, 29
Cooperative learning, 13–14
Corsaro, W., 54
Critical comprehension, 70
Critical discussions, 10
Cullinan, B., 10
Cultural diversity
  and cooperative learning, 13–14
  emphasis on, 26
  in group formation, 61
  and literature-based instruction, 12, 75–77
  within study groups, 21
Cultural values, and self-esteem, 12

Data analysis
  approach to, 55–57
  results of, 57–58
Data collection, 54
Delpit, L. D., 3, 12, 14
Developmental literacy theory, 5
Dewey, J., 8, 13
Dillon, D. R., 56
Directed Reading/Listening/Thinking Activity, 11
Direct instruction, 3
Disadvantaged children, 21, 77
Discipline, 68
Dodge, M., 9
Dramatic play, 11
Dramatic props, 9, 11, 25
Durkin, D., 7, 10, 18

Emotional handicaps, 14

Emotional maturity, 17
Engaged readers, 1, 14–15
Engagement perspective, 1
English as a Second Language (ESL), 71, 72
Ethnic diversity, *See also* Cultural diversity
  and cooperative learning, 13–14
  and literature-based programs, 75–77
  within study groups, 21
Experimental groups, 75
Expository material, 80–81

Farest, C., 10
Feedback, 76, 80
Felsenthal, H., 11
Feltboards
  in literacy centers, 25
  as props, 11, 75
  sample use of, 26
Fetterman, D. M., 55
Field, T., 9
Fielding, L. G., 16, 17, 19, 65
Fine motor control, 17
Firestone, W. A., 55, 56, 66
Ford, M. E., 6
Forman, E., 13
Form and function, in literacy processes, 19–20, 24
Free-choice time, 9, 16
Free reading, 36–37
Froebel, F., 7
Frost, J., 9
Frye, B. J., 19, 65

Galda, L., 34
Gambrell, L. B., 6, 7, 11
Gauthier, R., 60
Gender
  in group formation, 60
  within study groups, 21, 22
Girls, achievement of, 18
Golub, J., 67
Goodman, K. S., 1
Goodman, Y. M., 1
Graves, D. H., 65
Greaney, V., 16, 17, 18, 36, 45, 65
Green, J. L., 55, 60

Author

Lesley Mandel Morrow is a professor and Coordinator of the Early Childhood Elementary Graduate Programs at Rutgers Graduate School of Education. She received her Ph.D. from Fordham University in Curriculum and Supervision. She carries out research in classrooms in the areas of family literacy and early childhood literacy development and focuses on motivating interest in reading and writing, creating social collaborative environments to promote literacy development with children from diverse backgrounds.

Morrow has published numerous articles in national refereed journals such as *Reading Research Quarterly, Research in the Teaching of English, Journal of Reading Behavior, Reading Teacher,* and *Language Arts.* She has published ten books and numerous book chapters. Her most recent books are: *Literacy Development in the Early Years: Helping Children Read and Write* (3rd Edition) and *Family Literacy Connections in Schools and Communities.* She is a Principal Research Investigator for the National Reading Research Center and a member of the board of directors for the International Reading Association. She has received the Elva Knight Research Grant Award from the International Reading Association, and the National Council of Teachers of English Research Grant Award. She received Outstanding Research and Teaching Awards from Rutgers University, and the International Reading Association's Outstanding Teacher Educator of Reading Award. She also received an Outstanding Alumni Achievement Award from Fordham University where she received her Ph.D. Morrow can be contacted at Rutgers University, Graduate School of Education, New Brunswick, NJ 08903.

Titles in the NCTE Research Report Series

NCTE began publishing the Research Report series in 1963 with *The Language of Elementary School Children*. Volumes 4–6, 8–12, 14, 17, 20, and 21 are out of print. The following titles are available through the NCTE *Catalog*:

Vol. Author and Title

1   Walter D. Loban, *The Language of Elementary School Children* (1963)

2   James R. Squire, *The Responses of Adolescents While Reading Four Short Stories* (1964)

3   Kellogg W. Hunt, *Grammatical Structures Written at Three Grade Levels* (1965)

7   James R. Wilson, *Responses of College Freshmen to Three Novels* (1966)

13   Janet Emig, *The Composing Processes of Twelfth Graders* (1971)

15   Frank O'Hare, *Sentence Combining: Improving Student Writing without Formal Grammar Instruction* (1973)

16   Ann Terry, *Children's Poetry Preferences: A National Survey of Upper Elementary Grades* (1974)

18   Walter Loban, *Language Development: Kindergarten through Grade 12* (1976)

19   F. André Favat, *Child and Tale: The Origins of Interest* (1977)

22   Judith A. Langer and Arthur N. Applebee, *How Writing Shapes Thinking: A Study of Teaching and Learning*

23   Sarah Warshauer Freedman, *Response to Student Writing* (1987)

24   Ann DiPardo, *A Kind of Passport: A Basic Writing Adjunct Program and the Challenge of Student Diversity* (1993)

25   Arthur N. Applebee, *Literature in the Secondary School: Studies of Curriculum and Instruction in the United States* (1993)

26   Carol D. Lee, *Signifying as a Scaffold for Literary Interpretation: The Pedagogical Implications of an African American Discourse Genre* (1993)

27   James D. Marshall, Peter Smagorinsky, and Michael W. Smith, *The Language of Interpretation: Patterns of Discourse in Discussions of Literature* (1995)

PE1011 .N295 no.28
Motivating reading and writing in
diverse classrooms : social and
physical contexts in a literature-based
program / Lesley Mandel Morrow.